Illustrator
Ken Tunell

Editors
Dona Herweck Rice
Barbara M. Wally, M.S.

Editorial Project Manager
Ina Massler Levin, M.A.

Editor-in-Chief
Sharon Coan, M.S. Ed.

Art Director
Elayne Roberts

Associate Designer
Denise Bauer

Art Coordination Assistant
Cheri Macoubrie Wilson

Cover Artist
Larry Bauer

Product Manager
Phil Garcia

Imaging
Ralph Olmedo, Jr.
James Edward Grace

Researcher
Christine Johnson

Publishers
Rachelle Cracchiolo, M.S. Ed.
Mary Dupuy Smith, M.S. Ed.

The Seventies

Author

Mary Ellen Sterling, M.S. Ed.

Teacher Created Materials, Inc.
6421 Industry Way
Westminster, CA 92683
www.teachercreated.com

Reprinted, 2001
Made in U.S.A.

ISBN-1-57690-029-0

Table of Contents

Table of Contents *(cont.)*

Introduction

The 20th Century is a series which examines the political, economic, social, cultural, scientific, and technological changes and advances of the twentieth century and introduces students to the individuals who made history in each decade.

The Seventies chronicles America's changing role in world affairs following the Vietnam War. The political and social unrest of the late sixties carried over into the seventies. Antidraft and antiwar demonstrations continued on college campuses and in cities throughout the United States. Although peace talks between American Secretary of State Henry Kissinger and Le Duc Tho of Vietnam began in 1970, American involvement in the war in Vietnam continued until 1973.

In 1973 attention shifted to the world oil crisis. In the wake of the Arab oil embargo, gasoline prices rose sharply. As a result trade slumped, inflation rose, and large-scale unemployment hit harder than it had since the Great Depression. Some businesses failed.

The seventies also brought changes in American's attitudes and lifestyles. When the Watergate scandal exposed dishonesty at the highest level, the peace and love of the sixties gave way to anger and disappointment. Many turned inward, seeking individual fulfillment as they joined self-awareness groups or practiced meditation techniques. Natural foods and fabrics grew in popularity as the public became concerned about the environment. Although the 1970s were not as lively as the 1960s had been, they may have been more thoughtful. Some have called the seventies the "Me Decade," a time to "find one's self."

This unit includes the following:

- ☐ a time line—a chronology of significant events of the decade
- ☐ planning guides—summaries and suggested activities for introducing the key issues and events of the decade
- ☐ personality profiles—brief biographies of important individuals of the decade
- ☐ chronology—world events-of the decade
- ☐ language experience ideas—suggestions for writing and vocabulary building
- ☐ group activities—activities to foster cooperative learning
- ☐ topics for further research—suggestions for extending the unit
- ☐ literature connections—summaries of related books and suggested activities for expanding them
- ☐ curriculum connections—in math, art, language arts, social studies, and music
- ☐ computer applications—suggestions for selecting and using software to supplement this unit
- ☐ bibliography—suggestions for additional resources on the decade

To keep this valuable resource intact so that it can be used year after year, you may wish to punch holes in the pages and store them in a three-ring binder.

Time Line

	1970	1971
Politics and Economics	The United States invades Cambodia on April 30. Henry Kissinger begins secret peace talks in Paris with Le Duc Tho of North Vietnam. OSHA is established to provide safety guidelines for the workplace. The Environmental Protection Agency is established. The United States Post Office becomes independent.	The Twenty-sixth Amendment becomes law, lowering the voting age to 18. The Pentagon Papers reveal a government cover-up about Vietnam.
Social and Cultural	Four student antiwar protestors are killed at Kent State University by National Guard troops. The first Earth Day is celebrated. *Monday Night Football* debuts on ABC.	The Science of Sociobiology is Founded. During an uprising at Attica State Prison, 10 guards and 32 prisoners are killed. Cigarette ads are banned from television. Lieutenant Calley is court-martialed for the 1968 My Lai Massacre in Vietnam. Sun Myung Moon establishes the Unification Church in America. Amtrak service begins.
Science and Technology	Corning develops the fiber-optic cable for communications.	*Mariner 9* orbits Mars Astronauts of *Apollo 14* and *15* make trips to the moon. Engineers at Intel Corporation build the first commercial micro–processor. Pierre Verdon creates the food processor. Hoffman-LaRoche and Company of Switzerland introduce the LCD, short for Liquid Crystal Display. Canon markets the first pocket calculator. It prints the answers to problems on paper.

Time Line *(cont.)*

1972	1973	1974
President Nixon visits China, the first president to do so. Nixon is reelected. An FBI agent and four others are caught breaking into offices of the Democratic National Committee in the Watergate Building. United States and Canada sign an agreement to clean up the pollution in the Great Lakes.	President Nixon is inaugurated for a second term; Spiro Agnew is his vice president. The Senate opens the Watergate hearings. On October 10 Vice President Agnew resigns amid charges of tax fraud. Gerald Ford is selected as the new vice president. The United States and Vietnam sign a peace agreement in Paris.	President Nixon resigns; Gerald Ford becomes the thirty-eighth president with Nelson Rockefeller as his vice president. The Watergate hearings continue. President Ford pardons former President Nixon. Price and wage controls end. A bill is signed into law requiring 55 mph speed limits on all United States highways by March 2, 1974.
Life magazine ceases publication. On January 23 *Ms.* magazine debuts. Alabama Governor George Wallace is seriously wounded in an assassination attempt. Baseball players stage the first strike in the history of the game.	The last United States combat troops leave Vietnam. The military draft ends in the United States. Bonnie Tiburzi is the first female hired as a pilot for American Airlines and the first woman to fly for a commercial airline. Members of the American Indian movement occupy Wounded Knee, South Dakota, for 10 days. Billie Jean King defeats Bobby Riggs in the televised Battle of the Sexes tennis match. Pepsi Cola becomes the first American product licensed for sale in the Soviet Union.	Patty Hearst, 19-year-old daughter of wealthy publisher Randolph Hearst, is kidnapped by the SLA. *People* magazine debuts. Gasoline shortages cause long lines at gas stations. Mopeds are approved for use by the Department of Transportation.
The first home video games are introduced. Godfrey Hounsfield develops the CAT Scanner.	On May 14 NASA launches *Skylab*. The Internet, a method of linking computers, is developed by the Department of Defense.	UPC bar codes appear on food packages. The VCR is introduced.

Time Line *(cont.)*

1975	1976	1977
President Ford raises tariffs on oil imports. The United States bicentennial celebration officially begins on April 19. Former Teamster president Jimmy Hoffa disappears. John N. Mitchell, John D. Erlichman, and H.R. Haldeman are convicted and sentenced to 2½–8 years in prison for their roles in the Watergate cover-up.	Jimmy Carter is elected to the presidency.	James Earl Carter is inaugurated the thirty-ninth president of the United States; Walter Mondale is his vice president. The State Department agrees to admit 10,000 Vietnamese boat people into the country on an emergency basis. President Carter grants a pardon to draft evaders. The United States and Panama sign a canal treaty. The United States Department of Energy is established.
For the first time since 1950, Mauna Loa erupts in Hawaii. Two assassination attempts are made on President Ford in California. *Jaws*, directed by Stephen Spielberg, is the top grossing film to date.	The United States celebrates its bicentennial. Barbara Walters becomes the first female hired to anchor a network TV news program. In October the punk rock movement is launched. Reggae is popular. 200 contract legionnaire's disease at a convention in Philadelphia; 29 die. On September 18 members of Sun Myung Moon's cult travel to Washington, D.C., for a rally.	Elvis Presley dies. Gary Gilmore is executed, the first execution since 1967. A massive blackout in New York City leaves 9 million without electricity for up to 25 hours. The Trans-Alaska Pipeline begins to deliver oil from Valdez, Alaska, on July 28. *Star Wars* is released, becoming the most successful film of the decade.
The Heimlich maneuver is approved as an emergency treatment for individuals who are choking. Bill Gates and Paul Allen develop GW Basic, a language for programming computers.	The United States *Viking I* lands on Mars. Steven Jobs and Stephen Wozniak market the Apple computer. The first Cray computer, called the "supercomputer", is built.	First personal computers is developed. The two unmanned *Voyager* spacecraft are launched. The Magnetic Resonance Imaging (MRI) scanner is developed.

Time Line *(cont.)*

1978	1979	
President Carter hosts a Middle East peace conference at Camp David beginning September 6. Proposition 13, a measure to limit real estate taxes, is approved by Californians. Congress ratifies the Panama Canal Treaty. The United States and the People's Republic of China establish full diplomatic relations.	President Carter and Soviet Premier Leonid Brezhnev sign SALT II. Evangelist Jerry Falwell forms the "moral majority". President Carter reveals plans for the United States to use MX missiles. The Department of Education is established.	**Politics and Economics**
Congress extends the deadline for ratification of the Equal Rights Amendment from March 22, 1979, to June 30, 1982. More than 900 members of the People's Temple commit suicide in Jonestown, Guyana. Disco music and dancing are popular. The popular comic strip *Garfield* makes its debut.	Pope John Paul II visits the United States. The Sony Corporation markets the Walkman, a portable radio/tape player.	**Social and Cultural**
Louise Brown, the first test tube baby, is born.	Dr. Spenser Silver of the 3M Corporation develops Post-it Notes. On March 28 the Three Mile Island nuclear plant malfunctions and causes concern about the safety of nuclear power plants. *Skylab* breaks apart and lands in the Indian Ocean and in the Australian desert.	**Science and Technology**

Using the Time Line

Use pages five to eight to create a visual display for your classroom. Follow the steps outlined below to assemble the time line as a bulletin board display and then choose from the suggested uses those that best suit your classroom needs.

Bulletin Board Assembly

Copy pages five to eight. Enlarge and/or color them, if desired. Tape the pages together to form a continuous time line and attach it to a prepared bulletin board background or a classroom wall. (To make a reusable bulletin board, glue each page of the time line to oaktag. After the glue has dried, laminate the pages. Write on the laminated pages with dry erase markers.)

	1970	1971	1972	1973	1974
Politics and Economics	The United States invades Cambodia on April 30. Henry Kissinger begins secret peace talks in Paris with Le Duc Tho of North Vietnam. OSHA is established to provide safety guidelines for the workplace. The Environmental Protection Agency is established. The United States Post Office becomes independent.	The Twenty-sixth Amendment becomes law, lowering the voting age to 18. The Pentagon Papers reveal a government cover-up about Vietnam.	President Nixon visits China, the first president to do so. Nixon is reelected. An FBI agent and four others are caught breaking into offices of the Democratic National Committee in the Watergate Building. United States and Canada sign an agreement to clean up the pollution in the Great Lakes.	President Nixon is inaugurated for a second term; Spiro Agnew is his vice president. The Senate opens the Watergate hearings. On October 10 Vice President Agnew resigns amid charges of tax fraud. Gerald Ford is selected as the new vice president. The United States and Vietnam sign a peace agreement in Paris.	President Nixon resigns; Gerald Ford becomes the thirty-eighth president with Nelson Rockefeller as his vice president. The Watergate hearings continue. President Ford pardons former President Nixon. Price and wage controls end. A bill is signed into law requiring 55 mph speed limits on all United States highways by March 2, 1974.
Social and Cultural	Four student antiwar protestors are killed at Kent State University by National Guard troops. The first Earth Day is celebrated. *Monday Night Football* debuts on ABC.	The Science of Sociobiology is Founded. During an uprising at Attica State Prison, 10 guards and 32 prisoners are killed. Cigarette ads are banned from television. Lieutenant Calley is court-martialed for the 1968 My Lai Massacre in Vietnam. Sun Myung Moon establishes the Unification Church in America. Amtrak service begins.	*Life* magazine ceases publication. On January 23 *Ms.* magazine debuts. Alabama Governor George Wallace is seriously wounded in an assassination attempt. Baseball players stage the first strike in the history of the game.	The last United States combat troops leave Vietnam. The military draft ends in the United States. Bonnie Tiburzi is the first female hired as a pilot for American Airlines and the first woman to fly for a commercial airline. Members of the American Indian movement occupy Wounded Knee, South Dakota, for 10 days. Billie Jean King defeats Bobby Riggs in the televised Battle of the Sexes tennis match. Pepsi Cola becomes the first American product licensed for sale in the Soviet Union.	Patty Hearst, 19-year-old daughter of wealthy publisher Randolph Hearst, is kidnapped by the SLA. *People* magazine debuts. Gasoline shortages cause long lines at gas stations. Mopeds are approved for use by the Department of Transportation.
Science and Technology	Corning develops the fiber-optic cable for communications.	*Mariner 9* orbits Mars. Astronauts of *Apollo 14* and *15* make trips to the moon. Engineers at Intel Corporation build the first commercial micro-processor. Pierre Verdon creates the food processor. Hoffman-LaRoche and Company of Switzerland introduce the LCD, short for Liquid Crystal Display. Canon markets the first pocket calculator. It prints the answers to problems on paper.	The first home video games are introduced. Godfrey Hounsfield develops the CAT Scanner.	On May 14 NASA launches *Skylab*. The Internet, a method of linking computers, is developed by the Department of Defense.	UPC bar codes appear on food packages. The VCR is introduced.

	1975	1976	1977	1978	1979	
Politics and Economics	President Ford raises tariffs on oil imports. The United States bicentennial celebration officially begins on April 19. Former Teamster president Jimmy Hoffa disappears. John N. Mitchell, John D. Erlichman, and H.R. Haldeman are convicted and sentenced to 2½–8 years in prison for their roles in the Watergate cover-up.	Jimmy Carter is elected to the presidency.	James Earl Carter is inaugurated the thirty-ninth president of the United States. Walter Mondale is his vice president. The State Department agrees to admit 10,000 Vietnamese boat people into the country on an emergency basis. President Carter grants a pardon to draft evaders. The United States and Panama sign a canal treaty. The United States Department of Energy is established.	President Carter hosts a Middle East peace conference at Camp David beginning September 6. Proposition 13, a measure to limit real estate taxes, is approved by Californians. Congress ratifies the Panama Canal Treaty. The United States and the People's Republic of China establish full diplomatic relations.	President Carter and Soviet Premier Leonid Brezhnev sign SALT II. Evangelist Jerry Falwell forms the "moral majority". President Carter reveals plans for the United States to use MX missiles. The Department of Education is established.	Politics and Economics
Social and Cultural	For the first time since 1950, Mauna Loa erupts in Hawaii. Two assassination attempts are made on President Ford in California. *Jaws*, directed by Stephen Spielberg, is the top grossing film to date.	The United States celebrates its bicentennial. Barbara Walters becomes the first female hired to anchor a network TV news program. In October the punk rock movement is launched. Reggae is popular. 200 contract legionnaire's disease at a convention in Philadelphia; 29 die. On September 18 members of Sun Myung Moon's cult travel to Washington, D.C., for a rally.	Elvis Presley dies. Gary Gilmore is executed, the first execution since 1967. A massive blackout in New York City leaves 9 million without electricity for up to 25 hours. The Trans-Alaska Pipeline begins to deliver oil from Valdez, Alaska, on July 28. *Star Wars* is released, becoming the most successful film of the decade.	Congress extends the deadline for ratification of the Equal Rights Amendment from March 22, 1979, to June 30, 1982. More than 900 members of the People's Temple commit suicide in Jonestown, Guyana. Disco music and dancing are popular. The popular comic strip *Garfield* makes its debut.	Pope John Paul II visits the United States. The Sony Corporation markets the Walkman, a portable radio/tape player.	Social and Cultural
Science and Technology	The Heimlich maneuver is approved as an emergency treatment for individuals who are choking. Bill Gates and Paul Allen develop GW Basic, a language for programming computers.	The United States *Viking I* lands on Mars. Steven Jobs and Stephen Wozniak market the Apple computer. The first Cray computer, called the "supercomputer", is built.	First personal computers is developed. The two unmanned *Voyager* spacecraft are launched. The Magnetic Resonance Imaging (MRI) scanner is developed.	Louise Brown, the first test tube baby, is born.	Dr. Spenser Silver of the 3M Corporation develops Post-it Notes. On March 28 the Three Mile Island nuclear plant malfunctions and causes concern about the safety of nuclear power plants. *Skylab* breaks apart and lands in the Indian Ocean and in the Australian desert.	Science and Technology

Suggested Uses

1. Use the time line to assess students' initial knowledge of the era. Construct a web to find out what they know about the Iranian hostage crisis or the oil embargo, for example. Find out what they would like to know. Plan your lessons accordingly.
2. Assign each group of students a specific year. As they research that year, let them add pictures, names, and events to the appropriate area of the time line.
3. Assign the students to find out what events were happening around the world during the 1970s. Tell them to add that information to the bottom of the time line.
4. After adding new names, places, and events to the time line, use the information gathered as a study guide for assessment. Base your quizzes and exams on those people, places, and events which you have studied.
5. After the time line has been on display for a few days, begin to quiz students about the people, places, and events named on the time line. Call on one student at a time to stand so that he or she is facing away from the actual time line. Ask a question based on the information. *Variation:* Let the students compose the questions.
6. Use the time line as a springboard for class discussions; for example, what advances were made in the space program during this period? Who were some of the important feminists of the era? What impact did the oil embargo have on the automobile industry? What was the Watergate affair, who were some of the people involved, and what were their roles?
7. Divide the students into three groups and assign each group a different area: politics/economics, social/cultural, and science/technology. Have each group brainstorm important related people, places, and events that occurred during the seventies, and then create a group mural depicting these important happenings. Get permission to decorate a hallway wall or tape several sheets of butcher paper together to make a giant canvas.
8. Assign groups of students to make specialized time lines; for example, a time line of inventions, events in the women's rights movement, or advances in the space program.

Seventies Overview

- The political and social turmoil of the late 1960s continued into the seventies.
- American and South Vietnamese forces entered Cambodia and Laos in 1970 in an attempt to cut North Vietnamese supply lines.
- At Kent State University, students protesting the bombing of Cambodia set fire to an ROTC (Reserve Officers Training Corps) building. Called to stop the riot, National Guardsmen opened fire, wounding eight and killing four.
- In a new offensive North Vietnamese soldiers crossed into Quang Tri province, but they were stopped by the South Vietnamese. Bombing of North Vietnam by U.S. planes, halted in 1968, resumed in 1972 with railroads and supply lines as principal targets. The harbor at Haiphong was also mined.
- Although peace talks between Henry Kissinger of the U. S. and Le Duc Tho of North Vietnam began in Paris in 1970, fighting continued until a cease-fire agreement was reached in 1973.
- U.S. troops withdrew from Vietnam in 1973 and from Laos in 1974. In 1975 Saigon fell to the North Vietnamese. The same year, the communist Khmer Rouge came to power in Cambodia, and the Pathet Lao took over the government of Laos.
- In 1971 the publication of the Pentagon Papers, a history of the Vietnam War, added to antiwar sentiments by revealing that the government has not been completely honest.
- A court-martial convicted Lt. William Calley and sentenced him to life in prison for his role in the My Lai Massacre of 1968 in which 22 unarmed Vietnamese civilians were killed.
- Early in 1973 the trial of seven men accused of the 1972 break-in and wiretapping of the National Democratic Committee offices in the Watergate building began. Eventually this scandal spread to include members of the president's cabinet and staff and brought the threat of impeachment to President Richard Nixon.
- Spiro Agnew, accused of bribery, conspiracy, and tax evasion, resigned the vice presidency in October 1973. At his trial he pleaded *nolo contendre* and was fined and given probation.
- President Nixon named Gerald Ford, U.S. Representative from Michigan, to succeed Agnew. This was the first time the Twenty-fifth Amendment, passed in 1967, was applied.
- In 1974 Richard M. Nixon resigned the presidency. New president Gerald Ford nominated Nelson Rockefeller to fill the office of vice president.
- By 1976 people were quick to embrace Jimmy Carter with his homespun message of peace and hope as their new president.
- Revelations of misdeeds in government left the activists of the sixties frustrated and disillusioned. They turned their energies inward, embracing fitness, health foods, and transcendental meditation. Some have called the seventies the "Me Decade."
- Throughout the seventies, the women's movement grew stronger as leaders, including Gloria Steinem and Kate Millet, led the revolution. New opportunities were opened to women, and many left the safety of the home to find fulfillment in the workplace.
- In the 1973 landmark Supreme Court decision *Roe v. Wade*, women were granted abortion rights. A controversial topic, the debate has continued well into the nineties.
- The Arab oil embargo against the Western world had a severe effect on the economy. One effect was a new concern for the environment. Natural foods and fabrics gained popularity, and preventing air pollution and preserving the environment were important growing trends.

For Discussion

How has the women's movement impacted women's lives today?

Does an underlying distrust of the government linger in America today from the Watergate affair?

Is concern for the environment currently a major issue?

Introducing the Seventies

On this page you will find some interesting ways to introduce the seventies to the students. Keep in mind that these are suggestions only, and it is not necessary to use all of them. Your project selections should be based on student needs, interests, and objectives.

Disco Craze Disco music and fashions were popular during the 1970s. Display pictures of seventies fashions. Play disco music and learn how to do a disco dance (see instructions on page 16).

Literature Assign students to read some of the literature that was popular with young people in the seventies. Some suggested titles can be found in the Bibliography on page 95 and in the Literature Connections on pages 87–89. Discuss with the class the problems facing kids in the seventies and compare them to the typical problems of youths today.

Rock Stars Write a list of seventies rock stars on the board (see page 57 for some names). Ask students if they can identify any of them. Listen to some early music by David Bowie and Elton John. Discuss how their styles have changed since the seventies.

Twenty-sixth Amendment Discuss the Twenty-sixth Amendment and its importance (see page 19 for its complete text and a prepared activity).

America's Bicentennial Explain that the bicentennial of the Declaration of Independence, America's birthday, was celebrated in 1976. In New York City it was celebrated with tall ships in the harbor and a giant fireworks display at the Statue of Liberty. Divide the students into groups and let them plan one event anywhere in America that would symbolize the importance of Independence Day to the American people. For a prepared activity, see page 13.

Earth Day Environmental concerns were a major issue during the seventies. The first Earth Day was organized and celebrated on April 22, 1970. Have the class find out ways that their community celebrates Earth Day. See page 14 for a prepared activity.

Jogging During the seventies jogging and running marathons became popular sports. Weather permitting, take the class outdoors for a half-mile or longer jog.

Graffiti As the seventies progressed, graffiti became more commonplace. Logos, pictures, and words were spray-painted on walls, billboards, and advertising posters. Let students design their own graffiti. Attach a large sheet of white butcher paper to a classroom wall. Let students use markers or colored chalk to draw graffiti. No foul language or gang references allowed!

TV Television was more influential than ever, and shows about families were plentiful. Titles included *The Partridge Family, The Brady Bunch,* and *Happy Days*. Let students view an episode of a typical seventies family show and have them complete a TV Review, page 15. Discuss their responses in whole group.

Inventions Make a display of some of the seventies inventions—L'eggs stockings, Bounce fabric softener sheets, Clairol Herbal Essence shampoo, Mr. Coffee filters, Ziploc storage bags, etc. Cond' an informal poll to see which products can be found in the students' homes.

Discussing the Seventies

Create student interest with a lively discussion. Suggested topics and some methods for implementing them follow.

1. **Environment** One major issue of the seventies was the environment. A push was on for a global clean-up, and Earth Day was instituted on April 22, 1970. Discuss with the class present-day environmental concerns. Have student pairs make a list of ways they can contribute to keeping the environment clean. See page 14 for more on this topic.
2. **Women's Movement** The women's movement was in full swing throughout the seventies. Female activists lobbied for issues such as equal pay for equal work, and the Equal Rights Amendment was passed by both houses of Congress. With these events in mind, ask the students if they agree or disagree with this statement: The women's movement was the greatest social change of the seventies decade.
3. **ERA** With the class briefly review the provisions of the Equal Rights Amendment. Discuss possible reasons why the legislation was never ratified by the necessary number of states. Talk about current measures that have ensured equal rights for both sexes.
4. **Kent State** Review the events of the Kent State shooting. On May 2, 1970, student demonstrators were protesting the April 20, 1970, bombing of Cambodia. When they set fire to an ROTC building, the National Guard was called in. Two days later, on May 4, jittery guardsmen shot and killed four students; eight others were wounded. Conduct a class debate with one side defending the college students' actions and the other side defending the guardsmen's actions.
5. **Oil** In 1973 the Arab oil embargo led to skyrocketing gasoline prices, shortages, and rationing. Lines at gas pumps were long and tempers were short. This crisis led to the development of some important changes in road transportation, like compact cars with better fuel efficiency, lower maximum speed limits, etc. Discuss their influence on transportation today.
6. **Rock Music** During the seventies no one group stood out or dominated the charts like the Beatles had in the sixties. Instead, a number of different types of music became popular including glam rock, punk music, and reggae. Ask students to comment on the state of rock music today and how those earlier influences can be heard in some of the music of current stars.
7. **Sports** Favorite sports during the seventies included skateboarding, jogging, and disco roller-skating. Which of these sports are popular today among the students? Conduct a class poll of sports in which the students participate. Graph the results.
8. **Me Decade** The sixties was a period of optimism when anything seemed possible, and people believed that music, love, and peace could change the world. During the seventies people began to worry and reassess the events of the previous era. Disillusioned, they became more concerned with themselves and less concerned with their fellow humans. The seventies were labeled the "Me Decade" by some. Ask the class how they would characterize the present decade.

America's Bicentennial

On July 4, 1976, the United States of America celebrated a very special birthday—its 200th. To commemorate the historic occasion visitors flocked to Philadelphia where the Declaration of Independence was originally signed on July 4, 1776. As the Liberty Bell was struck at 2 P.M., church bells across the country also began chiming. Impurities in the casting of the Liberty Bell had caused it to crack on an earlier occasion, so a rubber mallet was used to strike it. However, the message of the bell was not muted.

To learn part of this message solve the problems below. Find the answers in the box and write the corresponding letter on the lines.

189÷21 450÷30 140÷7 60÷5 88÷4 96÷6 90÷3 85÷5

132÷6 120÷4 184÷8 224÷7 105÷7 320÷8 152÷4

160÷4 72÷4 120÷8 140÷7 114÷6 168÷8 162÷9

800÷40 76÷4 280÷7 200÷5 54÷3 160÷5

176÷8 112÷7 700÷28 168÷6

16 a	32 e	30 i	25 n	40 t
23 b	39 f	29 j	20 o	19 u
12 c	21 g	22 l	9 p	24 w
28 d	18 h	17 m	15 r	38 y

On Your Own

Find out how the Bicentennial was celebrated in New York City. Write a few sentences about it on the back on this page.

Earth Day

The first Earth Day was celebrated on April 22, 1970. Environmentalists conducted demonstrations and rallies across the nation to call attention to the growing problem of pollution. Today, the movement is still growing strong, and there is a bigger commitment than ever to protect the environment and to keep it clean.

On this page are a number of activities you can do to keep the spirit of Earth Day alive all year long. Complete at least two activities from the list below.

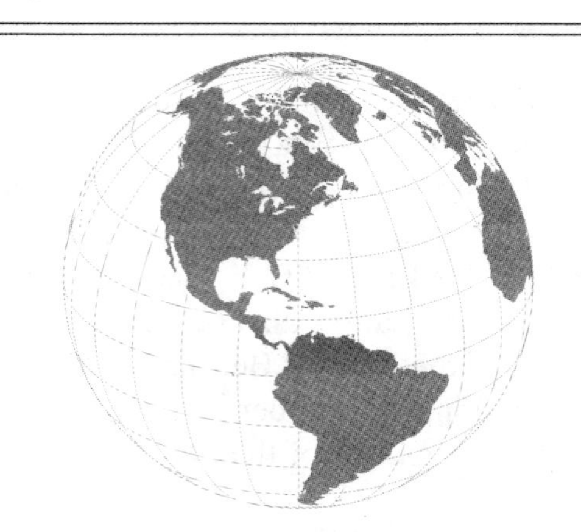

Suggested Activities

Learn Keep yourself informed about current environmental issues by reading articles in newspapers and magazines. Share what you have learned with members of your class and family.

Recycle I Think twice before throwing away paper that has only been used on one side. Save it and use it for scrap paper for math calculations, rough drafts, or even for doodling. When both sides have been used, deposit the paper into a recycling bin.

Recycle II Most items can be used a number of ways. Plastic margarine cups are a good example. Clean and save them for food storage, mixing paints, and storing small items such as paper clips. What other uses can you think of? Save other types of plastic, paper, and glass containers and think of new uses for them.

Save Water Be aware of how much water you waste and consume. Take shorter showers rather than baths. Turn the water off while you are brushing your teeth. Remind others in your household to follow the same guidelines.

Conserve To conserve electric lights, dust them regularly. Turn out the lights in a room when you or no one else is using them. In addition to conserving, you will also help your folks save money on the electric bill.

Save the Rain Forest Rain forests play a vital role in the biosphere. In addition to affecting worldwide weather, these forests absorb harmful carbon dioxide and help supply the Earth with oxygen. The rain forests are also our most important source of raw materials for creating new medicines. Help save the rain forests by writing to the Rainforest Action Network, 300 Broadway, Suite 28, San Francisco, CA 94133. Ask them what you can do to help.

Avoid Styrofoam Styrofoam, or polystyrene foam, is a nonbiodegradable material which means that it will never deteriorate—not even if it sits out in the sun or is buried in dirt for five hundred years. As much as possible, avoid using foam cups and plates. Remind your family to purchase eggs packed in paper cartons rather than foam containers.

Read There are plenty of good books out there to help you find ways to preserve and protect the environment. Take a look at *50 Simple Things Kids Can Do to Save the Earth* by The Earthworks Group (Andrews and McMeel, 1990) or ask your librarian to recommend some other titles.

TV Review

Name of Program ______________________________

1. Summary of episode ______________________________
2. Explain how the show depicts the mother. ______________________________

   ____
3. Explain how the show depicts the father. ______________________________

   ____
4. Name and describe a child who is a main character in the episode. ______________________________

   ____

   a. What problem or dilemma does he or she face in this episode? ______________________________

   ____

   b. How is it resolved? ______________________________
5. Name and describe a second child character. ______________________________

   ____

   a. How is he or she related to the other character you described? ______________________________

   ____

   b. What role did this character play in the main character's problem? ______________________________

   ____
6. Do you think the program portrays a realistic family? Explain your answer. ______________________________

   ____
7. How is your family like this TV family? ______________________________

   ____

   How is it different? ______________________________

   ____
8. Would you like to be a part of this TV family? Explain why or why not. ______________________________

   ____

Do a Little Dance

Discotheques, nightclubs that featured recorded music for dancing, became popular in the seventies. Teach students a basic disco dance. Make a transparency of the patterns and directions on this page for use on the overhead projector. Read them together and then demonstrate the steps to the class. Let students practice the steps without music. Then play a disco tune and do a little dance!

Boys

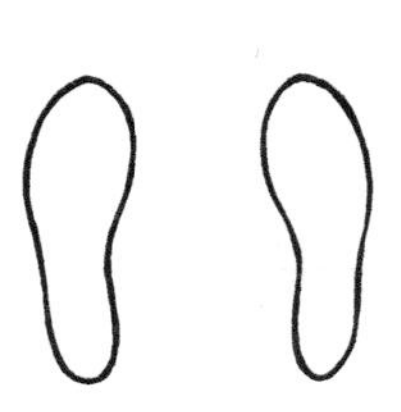

6. Step forward to your basic position and start the sequence over.

5. Bring the right foot next to the left foot and step together.

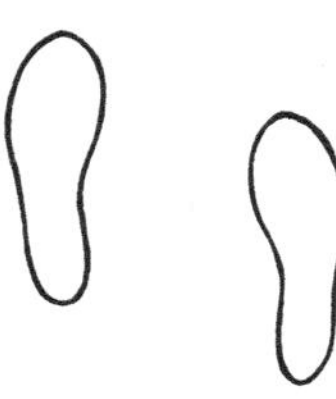

4. Now move your left foot in a diagonal movement in front of you.

3. As soon as your right foot is planted, touch your left foot next to it.

2. Touch your right foot next to your left and begin to move your right foot to the right on a diagonal.

1. Move your left foot to the left on a diagonal.

Basic Position: Both feet side by side, shoulder width apart

(Start Here)

Girls

6. Step forward to your basic position and start the sequence over.

5. Bring the left foot next to the right foot and step together.

4. Now move your right foot in a diagonal movement in front of you.

3. As soon as your left foot is planted, touch your right foot next to it.

2. Touch your left foot next to your right and begin to move your left foot to the left on a diagonal.

1. Move your right foot to the right on a diagonal.

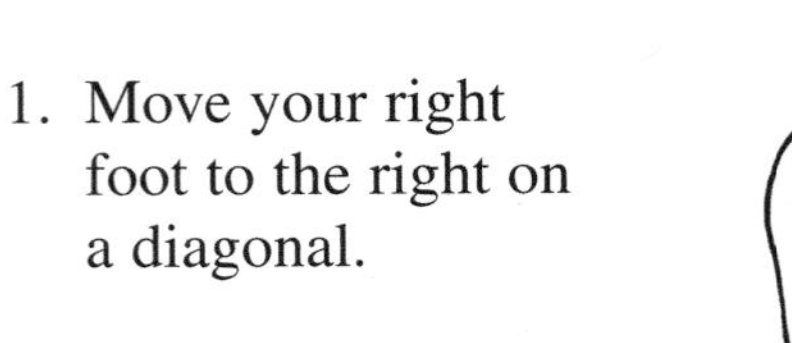

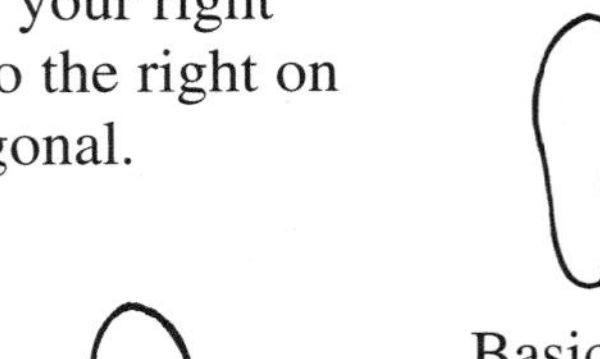

Basic Position: Both feet side by side, shoulder width apart

(Start Here)

Resource

Disco Dancing by Joetta Cherry and Gwynne Tomlan (Grosset and Dunlap, 1979)

Seventies Math

Many events of the seventies can be thought of as math problems, as seen in the samples below. To use this page with your class, make enough copies so that every pair of students will get one problem. Cut apart the rectangles and pass them out, one to each pair of students. Allow enough time for them to find a solution. In whole group, share the problems and discuss methods used to find answers.

1. In 1972 New York's World Trade Center became the tallest building in the world at 1,350 feet (412 m). Its twin towers rose 110 stories high. On average, how tall is each story? __________

   ____

2. Due to the oil embargo in 1973 gasoline prices doubled. If gas was 30 cents per gallon in the sixties, what was its price in 1973? ____

3. Patty Hearst's captors demanded a ransom of $70 worth of food for each needy Californian. The Hearst family responded with a $2 million food giveaway. How many persons were helped?

   ____

4. Mopeds were introduced in 1974. By 1977, 250,000 Americans had purchased mopeds. What is the average number of mopeds purchased each year during that period? ______________

   ____

5. Five million American people bought pet rocks in 1975. Each rock cost $5. Altogether, how much did Americans spend on pet rocks? ____

6. In 1975, 350 Transcendental Meditation centers nationwide served 600,000 people. What was the average number of people served by each center? ______________________________

7. During the 1976 Winter Olympics, the American speed skaters won six medals. There are eight events, each with three medals. Find the percentage of total possible medals received by Americans. ____

8. In 1975, 25 million people bought mood rings while five million people bought pet rocks. What percentage of the total purchases were made by people buying mood rings? ______________

   ____

9. Carole King's album *Tapestry* sold 13 million copies in 10 months. At that rate, how long would it take her to sell 39 million copies? ____

10. The World Trade Center was the world's tallest building at 1,350 feet (412 m) until it was surpassed by the Sears Tower at 1,454 feet (443 m). What is the difference in height between the two buildings? ____

11. Montreal budgeted $310 million for the 1972 Summer Olympics held there. The actual cost was $1.5 billion. What is the difference between the budgeted and actual costs? ______________

    ____

12. From 1954 to 1976 Hank Aaron hit an average of about 34 home runs per year. About how many home runs did he hit during his career? ____

Legislation of the 1970s

On this page you will find a list of some of the important legislation of the 1970s. A brief description is given for each one. Research further any topic that interests you.

1970 **EPA** The Environmental Protection Agency was established in July to help the nation control pollution of its air and water.

1971 **Wage and Price Freeze** A Pay Board was established to stop inflationary wage and salary increases. A Price Commission was set up to regulate price and rent increases.

Twenty-sixth Amendment On June 30 the voting age was lowered from 21 to 18. See page 19 for more information on this issue.

1972 **ERA** The Equal Rights Amendment called for complete legal equality between the sexes. It was passed by both houses of Congress but did not receive enough state support to be ratified.

Title IX Part of the Education Amendment Acts of 1972, Title IX forbade educational institutions which were receiving federal aid to discriminate on the basis of sex.

1973 **Roe v. Wade** In this still-controversial court case, the Supreme Court ruled that women have the right to obtain an abortion during the first three months of pregnancy. Anti-abortion rights activists continue to oppose and protest the decision on the basis of their belief that abortion is murder.

The Endangered Species Act This act placed a number of animals threatened with extinction on an endangered species list, thereby providing them with some protection for survival.

1974 **Speed Limits** All states were given until March 2, 1974, to comply with a 55-mph speed limit on U.S. highways or face the withdrawal of federal funding.

1975 **Metric System** A call was made for the voluntary switch to the metric system. Schools began teaching metrics, but adult resistance doomed the movement.

1977 **Panama Canal Treaty** President Carter and Panama's leader Omar Torrijos signed a treaty allowing the Panama Canal to be returned to Panama by the year 2000.

1978 **Bakke Case** In this Supreme Court ruling, it was determined that Allan P. Bakke was the victim of reverse discrimination and that racial quotas had kept the white student out of medical school. The court ruled out quotas but did permit affirmative action, giving extra consideration to minorities.

1978 **Camp David Accord** President Jimmy Carter, Egypt's President Anwar al Sadat, and Israeli Prime Minister Menachem Begin met for 12 days at Camp David to work out their political differences. On September 17, the leaders emerged from their talks to announce their agreement. Egypt became the first Arab nation to recognize Israel's right to exist.

For Discussion

Which pieces of legislation have had a lasting impact on Americans?

What is the most important piece of legislation to come out of the seventies?

The Twenty-sixth Amendment

On June 30, 1971, the Twenty-sixth Amendment to the Constitution was ratified. It lowered the voting age to eighteen. Read the complete text of this amendment below. Then answer the questions that follow. You may have to do some research to find answers.

Section 1. Right to Vote

The right of citizens of the United States, who are eighteen years of age or older, to vote shall not be denied or abridged by the United States or by any State on account of age.

Section 2. Enforcement

The Congress shall have power to enforce this article by appropriate legislation.

1. Write the provisions of this amendment in your own words. ______________________________

   ____

2. What events precipitated the passage of the Twenty-sixth Amendment? ______________________

   ____

3. The Fifteenth and Nineteenth Amendments also pertain to voting.

   What are the provisions of the Fifteenth Amendment? ______________________________

   ____

   What year was it ratified? ______________________________________

   What are the provisions of the Nineteenth Amendment? ______________________________

   ____

   What year was it ratified? ______________________________________

4. Consider all three voting amendments—the Fifteenth, Nineteenth, and Twenty-sixth.

   Who can vote in the United States? ______________________________________

   Who cannot vote in the United States? ______________________________________

5. Presidential elections are held every four years. With that in mind, determine in which Presidential election you will first be eligible to vote.

   year______________ your age______________

6. Do you think it is important to vote? Explain your answer. ______________________________

   ____

   ____

   ____

   ____

Make It Metric

When Congress called for a voluntary switch to the metric system in 1975, most adults balked at the idea. After all, they were used to buying milk in quarts and gallons. How would that compare to a liter? Another problem that would be faced immediately was the speed limit. If signs were suddenly changed to metric and speeds were expressed in kilometers, how many miles per hour would that be? The list of objections was lengthy and, in the end, even the schools seemed to forget about the metric system. Today in the United States metrics are relegated to a few pages in most math books.

To help you gain an understanding of how things are measured metrically, complete the hands-on activities below. You will need a small paper clip, a nickel, an empty one-quart bottle, and an empty one-liter bottle. If possible, both bottles should be of the same material—plastic, glass, or beverage cartons.

Take the small paper clip and place it on the outline at the right.

The paper clip is about one centimeter wide.

The wire used to make the paper clip is about one millimeter in diameter.

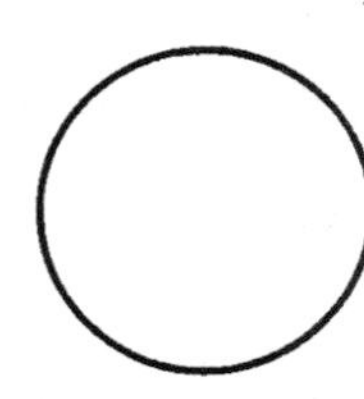

The paper clip has a mass of about one gram. Pick it up and place it in the palm of your hand to feel how light it is.

You will need the nickel for this exercise. Place it in the circle at right.

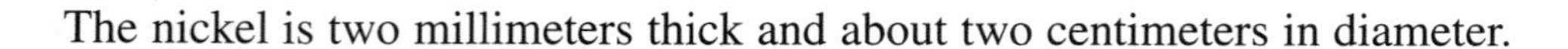

The nickel is two millimeters thick and about two centimeters in diameter.

The nickel has a mass of about five grams. Pick it up and place it in the palm of your hand. Remember how it feels. Remove the nickel and place the paper clip in your hand. Mentally compare the mass of the two objects.

Place the liter bottle and quart bottle next to one another. A liter contains 1,000 milliliters, and its volume is slightly greater than a quart.

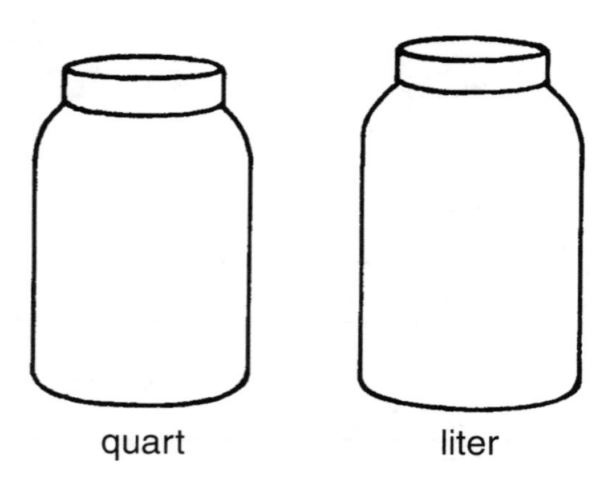

Fill both bottles with water. First pour the water from the liter into a large measuring cup and record the amount in the bottles at left. Now measure the amount of water from the quart bottle and record the amount. Compare the volume of the two containers.

Minimum Wage Math

The graph below illustrates the gradual rise of the minimum wage throughout the 1970s. From $1.60 per hour in 1970 the minimum wage reached $2.90 per hour in 1979.

Use the information from the graph to help you answer the problems that follow.

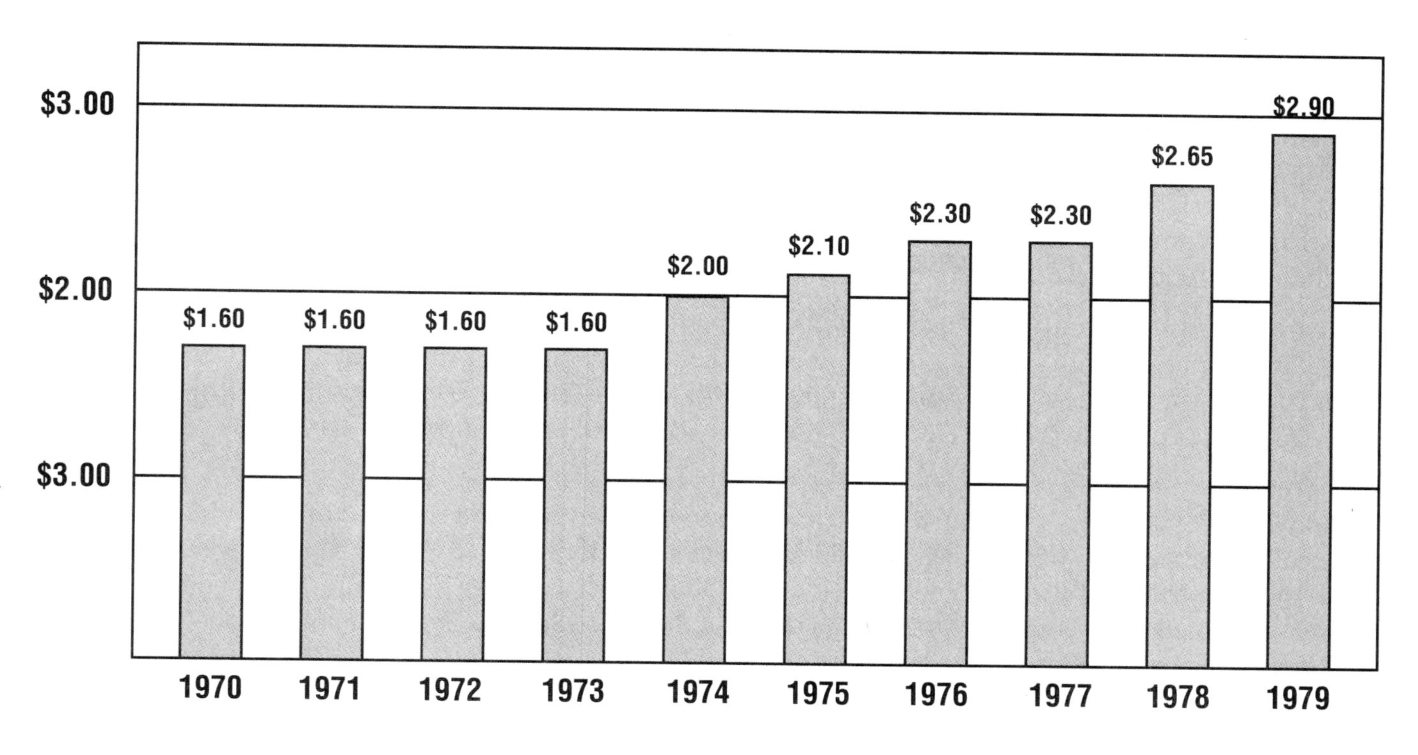

1. a. In which two-year period did the minimum wage remain the same? ____________________

   b. In which four-year period did the minimum wage remain the same? ____________________

2. a. In which two succeeding years was the amount of increase in the minimum wage the highest?

   ____

   b. In which two succeeding years was the amount of increase in the minimum wage the lowest?

   ____

3. a. How much did the minimum wage increase from 1970 to 1979? ____________________

   b. How much did the minimum wage increase from 1973 to 1978? ____________________

4. a. What was the annual average increase in the minimum wage rise during the seven-year period from 1973 through 1979? ____________________

   b. If the 1980 minimum wage was raised at the same rate as the average per year, what would the 1980 minimum wage be? ____________________

History of the Draft

The draft, or conscription for military service, in the United States began in colonial America. Over the course of time, changes were made in the way men were chosen and in the ages of those eligible for service. In the beginning of the 1970s, there was growing opposition to both the draft and the war in Vietnam. More and more frequently, protesters would gather and burn their draft cards in open defiance of the government. Organized violence against a draft system had occurred in 1863, but it did not compare to the actions taken by men in the seventies.

Throughout American history, a number of draft laws were passed to meet specific needs. Both the North and the South had their own conscription acts during the Civil War. In the North, men could avoid service by finding a substitute or paying the government $300. Between the Civil War and World War I, there was no conscription; but after World War I erupted, Congress passed the Selective Service Act. This law provided for eligible men between the ages of 18 and 45 to be chosen by a lottery system. Exemptions were allowed, but bounties were eliminated.

The period between World War I and World War II saw a return to the peacetime custom of maintaining a regular army along with National Guard units. When war broke out in 1939, the United States began a peacetime draft which was allowed to expire in 1947. Over the next 20 years, a number of draft laws were enacted. All of them required men to register with their local draft boards when they reached 18 years of age.

In January 1970, Congress instituted a lottery system with men between the ages of 19 and 20 eligible to be called for a period of one year. Previously, men were eligible for a period of seven years. The following year the draft was extended for two years, but after July 1, 1973, the draft was again left to expire. All young men continued to register with the Selective Service System until March 1975, when the lottery system was discontinued.

Since 1980, men aged 19 and 20 must register with the Selective Service, but they are not classified or inducted. The purpose of this registration is to compile names for a possible future military draft which would have to be approved by Congress.

In the box below is a sampling of draft classifications that were used during the years of active military conscription. Research and add two more classifications to the list.

1-A: Available for military service

1-A-O: Conscientious Objector; available for noncombat military service only

2-M: Deferred because of study preparing for a medical specialty

3-A: Deferred because of dependency of others

4-A: Has completed military service

4-F: Not qualified for military service

____

____

The Iranian Hostage Crisis

What events led to the Iranian hostage crisis? Why did it last so long? How was it finally resolved? These and other questions will be answered in the paragraphs that follow.

For years the United States had supported Iran politically and provided military assistance to help the country stave off Soviet expansion in the Middle East. The U.S. government's main reason for helping Iran was the importance of its rich oil supplies to the U.S. economy. In supporting Iran, the United States also supported its Shah, Mohammad Reza Pahlavi, until he was overthrown in 1979 by Islamic fundamentalists led by the Ayatollah Khomeini. The Shah's leadership had been cruel and authoritarian, and Iranians were resentful of him. After fleeing the country, the Shah went to Mexico where he became ill. He requested and was granted permission by the U.S. government to seek treatment at a New York City hospital. Not many days after that, on November 4, 1979, a mob of Islamic students attacked the U.S. embassy in Teheran and seized the staff. Although the action violated international law, the workers were held as hostages. The student radicals demanded that the Shah be returned to Iran in exchange for the release of the hostages, but President Carter refused. Fifty-two embassy workers were often blindfolded and paraded in front of television cameras while demonstrators chanted "Death to America."

Carter was not willing to submit to terrorism, so he tried diplomatic means to obtain the release of the hostages. First, he seized eight billion dollars' worth of Iranian deposits in U.S. banks and then ordered navy warships to the waters off Iran. Neither tactic worked, and public pressure continued to grow. In April 1980, over the protests of Secretary of State Cyrus Vance, President Carter gave permission for a rescue attempt. It was a disaster, however. Eight servicemen died when a transport plane collided with a helicopter. Vance resigned his office, and President Carter suffered a serious public image problem. The event also contributed to his stunning loss in the 1980 presidential election.

The hostage crisis was finally resolved on January 19, 1981, when Carter was able to negotiate the release of the hostages. It had been 444 days since they were first held in captivity, and, ironically, it was President Carter's last full day in office.

Suggested Activities

Respond If you were President Carter, what measures would you have taken to obtain the release of the hostages?

Research What became of the hostages after their release? How did their time in captivity affect them?

Richard Milhous Nixon

37th President, 1969–1974

Vice Presidents: Spiro T. Agnew, Gerald R. Ford

Born: January 9, 1913, in Yorba Linda, California

Died: April 22, 1994

Party: Republican

Parents: Francis Anthony Nixon, Hannah Milhous

First Lady: Thelma Patricia (Pat) Catherine Ryan

Children: Patricia, Julie

Nickname: Tricky Dick

Education: Duke University School of Law (ranked third in his class)

Famous Firsts:

- Nixon was the first president to resign from office.
- He was the first president to visit China.

Richard M. Nixon

Achievements:

- Nixon worked as a lawyer until 1946 when he won election to Congress.
- During his first year as president, the United States won the space race when *Apollo 11* astronaut Neil Armstrong became the first person to walk on the moon.
- Nixon proposed to end the Vietnam War with *Vietnamization* (replacing American troops with South Vietnamese soldiers). During the Vietnamization process, Nixon ordered an increase in the bombing of North Vietnam. In fact, more bomb tonnage was dropped on North Vietnam in this short period than on Germany, Italy, and Japan combined during all of WWII.
- On June 8, 1969, President Nixon announced that 25,000 U.S. soldiers would leave Vietnam by the end of August and 35,000 more by September 16.

Interesting Facts:

- Nixon was often accused of being paranoid. For example, he ordered his staff to keep a list of enemies, from politicians to businesspersons, athletes, and movie stars.
- Richard Nixon was born in a house built by his father.
- In 1968 Nixon's daughter, Julie, married David Eisenhower, grandson of former President Eisenhower.

Gerald Rudolph Ford

38th President, 1974–1977

Vice President: Nelson A. Rockefeller

Born: July 14, 1913, in Omaha, Nebraska

Party: Republican

Parents: Leslie Lynch, Dorothy King

First Lady: Elizabeth Anne (Betty) Bloomer Warren

Children: Michael, John, Steven, Susan

Nickname: Mr. Nice Guy

Education: University of Michigan (law degree)

Gerald R. Ford

Famous Firsts:

- Gerald Ford was the first president who had not been elected president or vice president.
- He was the first vice president to be selected under the Twenty-fifth Amendment to the Constitution which requires the president's choice to be confirmed by both houses of Congress.
- When Ford became president, he chose Nelson A. Rockefeller as vice president, and for the first time in American history neither the president nor the vice president had been elected.

Achievements:

- During World War II, Ford served with the Third Fleet in the South Pacific and earned the rank of lieutenant commander.
- He served 25 years in the House of Representatives and became minority leader in 1965.
- During his administration he introduced a program called Whip Inflation Now (WIN), but it failed to combat the growing recession.

Interesting Facts:

- Despite the fact that he was an excellent athlete (he had been a football star at the University of Michigan), he had a presidential reputation for clumsiness.
- Under his presidency, the nation suffered the worst unemployment and inflation rates since the Depression.
- Ford is one of 10 presidents to serve less than one term.
- President Ford legally changed his name from Leslie Lynch King, Jr., after his mother remarried and his stepfather, Gerald Ford, adopted him.

James Earl Carter, Jr.

39th President, 1977-1981

James E. Carter, Jr.

Vice President: Walter F. Mondale

Born: October 1, 1924, in Plains, Georgia

Party: Democrat

Parents: James Carter and Lillian Gordy

First Lady: Eleanor Rosalynn Smith

Children: John, James Earl III, Jeffrey, Amy

Nickname: Hot

Education: U.S. Naval Academy

Famous Firsts:

- He was the first president to be born in a hospital.
- Jimmy Carter was the first president elected from the Deep South since before the Civil War.

Achievements:

- He served in the navy during World War II.
- After his father died, Jimmy Carter resigned from the navy, and he and his wife, Rosalynn, worked in the family's peanut-farming business.
- He was elected to the Senate in 1952.
- In 1966 he ran unsuccessfully for governor of Georgia. In 1970 he was elected governor of the state.
- The Department of Energy and the Department of Education were created under his administration.
- He conducted the Camp David accords in 1978, bringing about peace between Israel and Egypt.
- President Carter pardoned the Vietnam draft evaders.

Interesting Facts:

- Carter was a speed-reader who could read over 2,000 words per minute with 95 percent accuracy.
- When he traveled, President Carter often carried his own luggage.
- Carter left office as one of the most unpopular presidents in history, yet he became one of the nation's most successful and active ex-presidents.
- His best remembered foreign relations event was the Iranian hostage crisis. On his final full day in office, the hostages were released.
- Jimmy Carter and his wife, Rosalynn, currently serve as regular volunteers for Habitat for Humanity, a program which develops and builds housing for low-income families.

A Presidential Quiz

Test your knowledge of the three 1970s presidents with this quiz. Read the words, events, and names in each row. Determine which president is most connected with them. Circle the N for Nixon, F for Ford, or C for Carter.

1. N F C Watergate, Arab oil embargo
2. N F C Twenty-sixth Amendment passed, visit to China
3. N F C Iranian hostage crisis, Department of Energy created
4. N F C United States bicentennial, North and South Vietnam reunify
5. N F C Camp David peace talks, Three Mile Island accident
6. N F C Supreme Court case *Roe v. Wade*, Vietnamization
7. N F C pardoned Nixon, Nelson Rockefeller was vice president
8. N F C human rights, gas shortages
9. N F C boycott of Moscow Olympics, Walter Mondale
10. N F C foreign policy was détente, Equal Rights Amendment
11. N F C boat people, moral majority
12. N F C Kent State shootings, James McCord
13. N F C *Viking I* is launched, granted a presidential pardon to his predecessor
14. N F C silent majority, faced impeachment
15. N F C Panama Canal Treaty, Secretary of State Cyrus Vance
16. N F C Bakke Case decided by Supreme Court, Salt II agreement
17. N F C first Earth Day celebrated, resigned from office
18. N F C Whip Inflation Now campaign, Vietnam war ends
19. N F C gave aid to Sandanistas, energy crisis
20. N F C Saturday Night Massacre, Vice President Agnew resigns

---

Teacher Note (*fold over before copying*)

Presidential Chart Draw a three sectioned chart on the chalkboard or make one for the overhead projector. Label each section with a different president's name. As you read aloud each of the above items, call on a student to go to the board and make a check mark in the correct presidential column.

Answers: 1. N 2. N 3. C 4. F 5. C 6. N 7. F 8. C 9. C 10. N 11. C 12. N 13. F 14. N 15. C 16. C 17. N 18. F 19. C 20. N

Three First Ladies

During the 1970s there were three First Ladies: Pat Nixon, Betty Ford, and Rosalynn Carter. Each had a distinctive personality and brought a different flare to the White House. Read the short biographies that follow and complete one of the activities at the bottom of the page.

Pat Nixon When Pat Nixon became First Lady, she was the mother of two teenage daughters, Tricia and Julie. Continuing in the tradition of Jackie Kennedy, Mrs. Nixon proceeded with the renovation of the White House to make it a museum of American heritage. In addition, she supported the cause of volunteerism and urged Americans to get involved with their communities. Her greatest political success was as a goodwill ambassador on trips to Africa. Pat Nixon died in 1993 and is buried beside her husband in Yorba Linda, California, at the Richard Nixon Library and Birthplace.

Betty Ford Betty Ford is most remembered for her candidness in her personal life. When she spoke publicly about her battle with breast cancer, she raised public awareness of the disease and served as an inspiration to others who faced cancer. As First Lady, Betty Ford also supported the Equal Rights Amendment and valued both the traditional role of women and the role of women in the workplace. After leaving the White House, Mrs. Ford publicly described her struggle with addiction to alcohol and pain medication, and she founded the Betty Ford Clinic for substance abuse in Rancho Mirage, California.

Rosalynn Carter When Jimmy Carter was president, his wife Rosalynn served as his most trusted advisor and represented him officially during a trip to Central and South American countries. She sometimes sat in on cabinet meetings where she quietly took notes. These acts aroused much criticism, but there were those who admired her. Rosalynn's own agenda included supporting mental health reform, actively supporting legislation to reform Social Security, and urging approval of the Equal Rights Amendment. A woman of action, Rosalynn believed firmly in the necessity of women pursuing careers outside the home.

Suggested Activities

History Make a chart of the childhoods and educations of these three First Ladies.

Comparison Construct a three-way Venn diagram comparing the accomplishments and roles of these First Ladies.

First Ladies Explain how each of these three women changed and impacted the role of First Lady for future First Ladies.

Election Facts

	Election of 1972	Election of 1976
Democrats	South Dakota Senator George McGovern, a liberal, was the Democratic choice for president. He first selected Thomas Eagleton of Missouri as his vice president but changed to Sargent Shriver when it was announced that Eagleton had received shock treatments for depression.	Jimmy Carter, former governor of Georgia, was a relative unknown in the political arena but his informal style and big, toothy smile helped him win a first ballot victory at the Democratic convention. He talked about restoring people's faith in the government.
Republicans	Richard Nixon and Spiro Agnew easily won their party's renomination. Fewer than 25,000 troops remained in Vietnam, and Nixon campaigned on his record for negotiating peace with the communists.	Despite a run by former California governor Ronald Reagan, President Ford took the Republican nomination. Nelson Rockefeller would continue as the vice presidential nominee.
Other	Alabama's George C. Wallace, who broke with the Democrats in 1968 to run as the American Independent Party candidate, sought the Democratic nomination. He withdrew after he was shot while campaigning in May.	
Slogans		Some of Ford's campaign buttons read, "I'm Voting for Betty's Husband." Another campaign slogan was "Whip Inflation Now" or "WIN."
Issues	McGovern charged that Nixon's administration was the most corrupt in U.S. history. He promised an immediate and complete withdrawal of American troops from Vietnam and was critical of government cuts in spending. He suggested an income tax increase might be necessary in the forthcoming years.	Carter and Ford held two debates. At the second one, which was held in October, Ford mistakenly claimed that Poland was free of Soviet domination. The error hurt him and most likely lost him the race. Carter, in the meantime, promised more jobs, welfare, and tax reform.
Winner	Nixon won by a margin of nearly 20 million votes. He won 49 states, losing only in Massachusetts and the District of Columbia. Nixon's electoral vote total was 520 to McGovern's 17.	It was a very close election with Carter winning by 2 percent of the popular votes. This election was notable for its low voter turnout. Carter garnered 297 electoral votes to Ford's 240.

Election Figures

Make a copy of this page for each pair of students. Instruct them to answer the questions using the information from the chart below.

Year	Candidate	Popular Votes	Electoral Votes
1972	Nixon	47,167,319	520
	McGovern	29,168,509	17
	Others	1,178,238	1
1976	Carter	40,828,587	297
	Ford	39,147,613	240
	Others	1,575,459	1

1. In which year was the difference in popular votes between the top two candidates the greatest?

   What was the margin? ______________________________
2. What percent of the electoral votes did Nixon carry in the 1972 election? ______________
3. How many more popular votes did Carter have than Ford in the 1976 election? ____________
4. Was the total number of electoral votes the same or different in the 1972 and the 1976 elections?

   ____

   How many total electoral votes were there in each election ? ______________
5. In which election was the greatest total number of popular votes cast?______________

   What is the difference between the total number of popular votes cast in 1972 and 1976?

   ____
6. What percentage of the total number of electoral votes did Ford have in 1976?______________
7. Complete the bar graphs to compare electoral votes in each election.

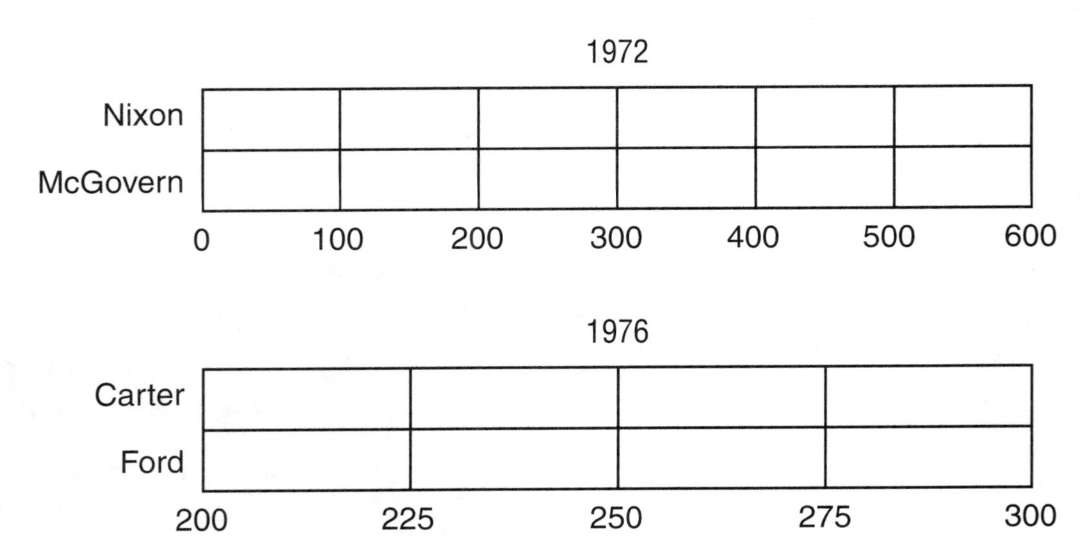

The Watergate Affair

On this and the next page you will find a step-by-step explanation of the Watergate affair. Make a copy of both pages for each group of students. After reading the text together, have students complete the activities at the bottom of the next page.

1. The setting is two o'clock in the morning on Saturday, June 17, 1972, at the Democratic headquarters in the Watergate building complex. Five suspected burglars are arrested there. The burglars are attempting to adjust the bugs they had previously installed in order to listen in on Democrats as they planned their strategy for the upcoming election. All five men are wearing surgical gloves and armed with walkie-talkies. Their tools, false identification, telephone tapping devices, money, film, and cameras are confiscated by the police.

2. One of those arrested is James W. McCord, security chief for the Committee for the Reelection of the President. The organization is headed by John N. Mitchell, a former U.S. Attorney General in Nixon's cabinet. Mitchell has resigned that post so that he can manage the president's re-election. He denies any wrongdoing or White House involvement.

3. Two reporters for the *Washington Post*, Bob Woodward and Carl Bernstein, are assigned to investigate the allegations. They find out that the break-in has been directed by G. Gordon Liddy, a former FBI agent, and E. Howard Hunt, a former CIA agent.

4. On August 29, 1972, President Nixon declares that no one in his administration is responsible for Watergate. Furthermore, John Dean, an attorney on his staff, has conducted an investigation clearing all White House staff of any wrongdoing.

5. Nixon wins the 1972 presidential election by an overwhelming majority.

6. On January 8, 1973, with Judge John Sirica presiding, the trial of G. Gordon Liddy, E. Howard Hunt, and the five burglars is under way. Sirica is dissatisfied with the questioning and delays sentencing.

The Watergate Affair *(cont.)*

7. On February 7, 1973, the U.S. Senate creates a Senate Select Committee to investigate Watergate more thoroughly. Sam Ervin, a Democratic senator from North Carolina, is chosen to head the committee.

8. In a written statement, McCord reveals that White House officials had conducted a cover-up to hide their involvement and that they had been pressured to plead guilty while not revealing what they knew. With that revelation, the White House cover-up begins to unravel. John Mitchell admits lying, and John Dean, President Nixon's attorney, accuses Nixon's closest advisor of participating in Watergate. H. R. Haldeman, President Nixon's chief of staff, and John Ehrlichman, a top presidential advisor, are also implicated. President Nixon continues to maintain his innocence.

9. On May 17, 1973, televised hearings of Watergate begin. It is discovered that secret audiotape recordings have been made of Nixon and his aides as they conferred about Watergate. At first President Nixon refuses to supply the tapes, but he finally releases some of them. One tape contains an 18-minute gap that has intentionally been erased. Another tape made on July 23, 1972, clearly proves that Nixon had conspired with his aides to undermine the FBI investigation.

10. The House Judiciary Committee votes to impeach President Nixon, but he resigns on August 8, 1974, before they can take action.

Suggested Activities

Complete these activities on another sheet of paper. Be prepared to discuss your responses with the other groups in the class.

1. Respond in writing to the following statement: Although the Watergate scandal left the country in great turmoil, it proved that the American system of government works.
2. Watergate can be described as Nixon's worst moment and the event for which he is most identified in history. However, he did take some positive actions. What were some highlights of his presidency?
3. Research and find out what became of Dean, Haldeman, Ehrlichman, and Liddy. Write three or four sentences about each one's career following his incarceration.

The Watergate Players

How well do you know the people involved in the Watergate affair? To find out, choose a partner and cut apart the rectangles below. Match the Watergate figures with their roles in the scandal. Check your answers with your teacher when you are through matching.

1. John Dean	2. James McCord	3. John Ehrlichman	4. Sam Ervin
5. H. R. Haldeman	6. Archibald Cox	7. G. Gordon Liddy	8. John Mitchell
a. This former CIA agent was working for the Committee for the Reelection of the President when he and four others were arrested at the Watergate building.	b. He served as counsel to the president; his job was to cover up the Watergate fallout and any White House connection to the break-in.	c. A former United States attorney general, he was the mastermind of the whole Watergate operation.	d. The Watergate hearings were chaired by this senator who insisted on public hearings conducted by his committee.
e. Appointed special prosecutor by Nixon, he was fired after finding evidence showing Nixon was involved in the cover-up.	f. Chief adviser on domestic affairs and one of Nixon's top aides, he resigned before the Senate public hearings began.	g. This chief of staff destroyed many documents that connected the White House with the men who had planned the break-in.	h. One of the five burglars caught in the Watergate break-in, he was a lawyer for the Committee for the Reelection of the President.

The Oil Crisis

Read the paragraphs about the events which led to the Arab oil embargo and its effects on the U.S. economy. On a separate sheet of paper, answer the questions that follow.

The creation of the state of Israel on May 14, 1948, angered Arab nations because this new state was composed of land claimed by both Arabs and Jews. Over the years that followed, Arabs and Israelis launched several attacks and counterattacks against one another. On October 6, 1973, the Jewish holiday of Yom Kippur, the Arab states attempted once again to destroy Israel. A massive United States-backed airlift of supplies aided Israeli defenders and incensed the Arabs. In an unparalleled show of unity, the Arab states retaliated by using their vast oil resources as an economic weapon. On October 17, 1973, they declared an embargo on all oil shipments to Europe and North America.

Almost immediately, the affected countries were impacted by the strict measure. In the United States, a number of energy-saving measures were instituted. Some gas stations began closing on Sundays, speed limits were lowered, and rationing systems were installed. Buyers began to look more closely at foreign-made cars which were smaller and consumed less gas than their American counterparts. Petroleum-based products doubled in price, and research of alternate energy sources was stepped up.

The United States and other countries quickly realized that they could no longer depend on the Middle East for an inexhaustible supply of cheap oil. Although the Arabs lifted the oil embargo on March 18, 1974, oil prices remained high, nearly double what they had been just a year prior.

Suggested Activities

Knowledge Identify three energy-saving measures which were instituted as a result of the Arab oil embargo.

Comprehension In your own words, describe the events that led up to the Arab oil embargo against the Western world.

Application Predict how Americans reacted to news of the oil embargo and what inconveniences bothered them the most.

Analysis Draw conclusions about the impact that the oil embargo had on the auto industry and identify what changes were made in U.S. automobiles as a result of the embargo.

Synthesis Propose your own ideas for energy-saving measures that could be employed in case of another oil embargo.

Evaluation Assess the impact of the oil embargo on our present economy, or determine which of the energy-saving measures instituted in 1973 have left positive, long-term effects on the economy.

The Oil Crisis Elsewhere

When the oil-producing nations founded OPEC, the Organization of Petroleum Exporting Countries to control production and prices, the soaring price of oil brought great wealth to traditionally poor countries. It became very common to see rich Arabs spending their money freely in Western countries. See page 36 for more information on OPEC.

While the Arabs were busy spending their newly earned riches, people in other countries were suffering adversely. In Great Britain, for example, the crisis was compounded by a shortage of coal supplies, and industry had to be limited to three days a week to conserve the electricity supply. Oil-based synthetics and plastics increased in price throughout the world. People began to appreciate the important role that petroleum had on their lives.

Hundreds of everyday objects are made from petroleum and its by-products or contain petroleum in some form. Below you will find the names of 25 things that are petroleum-based. Find and circle the names of all 25 items in the wordsearch puzzle.

paint
gasoline
plastic
fertilizer
inks
pantyhose
appliances
tools
hydrogen peroxide
ammonia
detergents
kerosene
asphalt
tar
benzene
rubber tires
vinyl records
clothing
petroleum jelly
lubricants
soaps
insecticides
paraffin
footwear
furniture

H X U P J L V S L G X D M I D P X I E B
I Y F E R T I L I Z E R N B E N Z E N E
I R D T N U N S Q K H S N F I J X Q W R
B Z E R S I Y L E P E Y U F D N W V R M
M R T O O E L L D C L R F Q V J S F M I
S A E L A G R O T V N A O I P L L K M O
M P R E P O E I S I R A S S X N C K S C
O V G U S V C N T A R E I T E O K L B D
C Q E M M I O U P R G P D L I N D V U S
O Y N J D E R P B E E U U J P C E R B Z
J Y T E P E D P Z U R B O H H P Z E N S
M C S L A C S R K A R O B Q O L A O S V
Y G K L N S G W E I H C X U J R K I G Z
R V N Y T L Z W C N A I G I R K C X N D
G D I I Y O T A D O S N U J D A R L K T
S Z D A H O N X S M P A H M J E T C A Y
Q R I P O T P V B M D K D H O A S V L G
P L X F S J O T L A H P S A N P P S C N
Z D X N E F T L R H W E G N M R P Z Q A
J M I G O Y C R C K T G J I T T L U H H

OPEC

In the 1950s, oil production exceeded the demand, and prices dropped. OPEC, the Organization of Petroleum Exporting Countries, was founded in 1960 by the world's primary oil exporters—Saudi Arabia, Kuwait, Iran, Iraq, Venezuela, Algeria, Ecuador, Gabon, Indonesia, Libya, Nigeria, Qatar, UAE (the United Arab Emirates), and Venezuela—to control the supply of oil and the price paid to its members. Due to competition from non-OPEC oil producers, prices remained low until the 1970s. An increase in the demand for oil and the depletion of other sources allowed OPEC to raise prices. In 1973 the organization reduced their production and began an embargo against certain countries as a protest against the Arab-Israeli War. Although the cutback represented less than seven percent of the world supply, panic ensued and oil prices skyrocketed. When OPEC members realized the full extent of their control, they kept oil prices high, even after the boycott. They also controlled how much oil was—or was not—produced.

In 1978 Iran, under the new leadership of the fundamentalist Islamic Ayatollah Khomeini, cut off oil exports and a mild oil shortage ensued. One year later, OPEC announced another steep price increase, but it was overshadowed by another situation—the Iranian hostage crisis.

Thirteen countries are members of OPEC. Most of them are located in Africa or the Middle East. Label the countries of Algeria, Libya, Nigeria, Gabon, Iran, Iraq, Kuwait, Saudia Arabia, and Qatar on the map below.

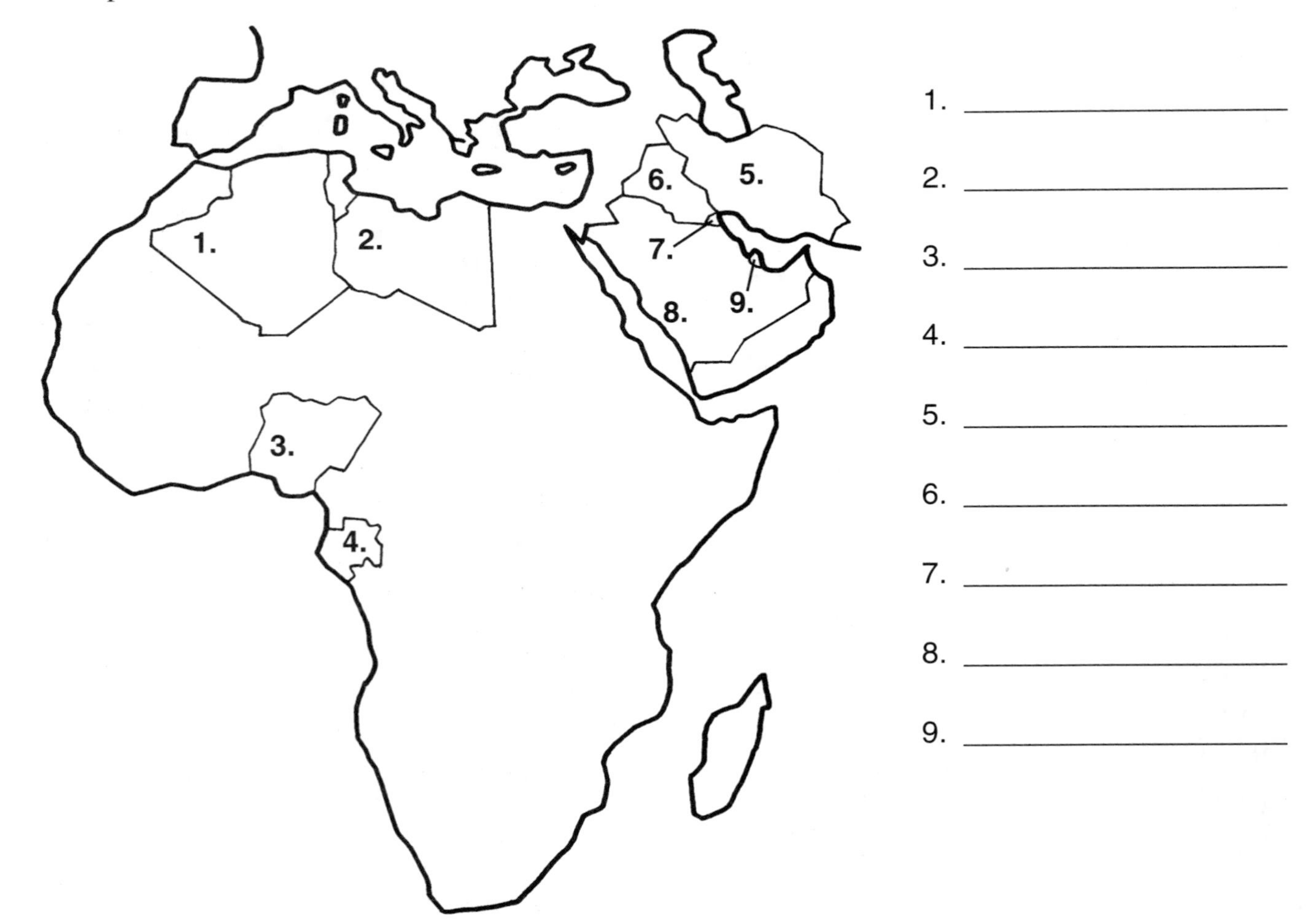

1. ______________________

2. ______________________

3. ______________________

4. ______________________

5. ______________________

6. ______________________

7. ______________________

8. ______________________

9. ______________________

Feminists of the Seventies

The women's movement was probably the greatest social change of the seventies decade. At the helm of this movement was Gloria Steinem, the leading feminist and proponent of women's rights during the era. Ms. Steinem was not alone in her fight, however. Some other leading figures of women's liberation included Betty Friedan, Bella Abzug, and Shirley Chisholm. Below, you can read about each of these women and her role in the feminist cause.

Gloria Steinem

Gloria Steinem Despite an impoverished and insecure childhood, Gloria Steinem was able to attend Smith College from which she graduated magna cum laude. Instead of studying the traditional literature and art, Steinem majored in government. After graduation she went to India on a two-year scholarship. When she returned to the United States, she worked in journalism. In 1972 Ms. Steinem and 13 other women published the first issue of *Ms.* magazine. Her articles and personal appearances helped build feminism into a national movement.

Bella Abzug Bella Savitzky Abzug was born on July 24, 1920, into a loving family, but tragedy struck early in her life when her father died suddenly. Barely 13, she felt the loss deeply. At school she earned a reputation as a political activist, and it was no surprise when she decided to pursue a law degree. Even her marriage to Martin Abzug did not deter her. After graduating from Columbia University, Bella Abzug joined a law office specializing in labor union cases. Over the years she took up a number of social causes and in 1970 decided to make a bid for a seat in Congress. After an aggressive campaign, she won a seat in the House of Representatives. She worked for the passage of the Equal Rights Amendment and, with Shirley Chisholm, sponsored a bill for federal support of day-care centers for the children of working mothers. Considered a radical by some, Ms. Abzug maintained that she was merely an idealist who was fighting for the ordinary man and woman.

Shirley Chisholm

Shirley Chisholm After she earned a master's degree in education from Columbia University, Shirley Chisholm worked in New York City's day-care system. Angered by the inequalities that African American women and children faced, she entered politics in 1964 in an effort to get government support for them. She became the first black woman elected to the U.S. Congress. For 14 years Ms. Chisholm served as a U.S. Representative. She supported the Equal Rights Amendment and helped found the National Women's Political Caucus.

Feminists of the Seventies *(cont.)*

Betty Friedan During the 1960s, Betty Friedan wrote *The Feminine Mystique*, in which she questioned the traditional role of women in society. Like Gloria Steinem, Friedan had studied at Smith College and worked as a journalist before becoming involved in feminism. In 1966 she founded the National Organization for Women, or NOW. NOW worked to achieve equal rights for women and is still an active force in society and politics. Friedan joined with Gloria Steinem, Bella Abzug, and Shirley Chisholm to found the National Women's Political Caucus in 1971.

Betty Friedan

Complete the chart below by checking all that apply. Some possible resources for you to explore are listed at the bottom of this page.

Achievements	Gloria Steinem	Betty Friedan	Bella Abzug	Shirley Chisholm
Graduated from College				
Worked in Journalism				
Wrote One or More Books				
Founded a Feminist Organization				
Promoted Equal Rights for Women				
Was/Is Active in Politics				
Served in Congress				

Resources

Focus on Women (Teacher Created Materials, #495)

Herstory: Women Who Changed the World by Ruth Ashby and Deborah Gore Ohrn (Viking, 1995)

Is There a Woman in the House . . . or the Senate? by Bryna J. Fireside (Albert Whitman & Company, 1994)

Marian Wright Edelman

Growing up in the Wright household meant doing chores, getting good grades in school, and helping others in the community. These were lessons that Marian Wright learned well and brought with her when she took up the social cause of children's rights.

Marian Wright Edelman

Wright grew up with her siblings in a segregated neighborhood. Her father, Arthur, worked hard to make their community a better place to live. When black children were not allowed to play in the white park, for example, he built a playground behind his church. Although Arthur Wright died when his daughter was only fourteen, she never forgot his concern for others.

After graduating from high school in 1956, Wright attended Spelman College, the first college for black women in the nation. The civil rights movement was just beginning, and she wanted to be part of it. While working for the NAACP in Atlanta, she decided to become an attorney. In 1963 Wright graduated from Yale Law School, and after passing the bar, she began to defend many civil rights cases. She also began devoting time to the Head Start programs in Mississippi. After marrying Peter Edelman in 1968, she wrote a report about the government's failure to help poor children get a good education. It made headlines but failed to bring about any action. Her next step was to organize a group that included church groups, women's organizations, and the National Education Association. Together they would propose bills that would provide help for children. In 1973 the group was expanded into the Children's Defense Fund (CDF) which would look out for the needs of all children in the United States, but particularly poor children. Today, Marian Wright Edelman continues to be active in the CDF. She has received numerous honors for her tireless work on behalf of American children.

Suggested Activities

Children's Defense Fund The CDF is a nonprofit organization dedicated to the betterment of all children. Funded by individual donations and corporations, the CDF actively sponsors research, publicity, public education, legislation, and advocacy programs on children's issues. Since its inception in 1974 the organization has been responsible for the passage of the Education for All Handicapped Children Act of 1974, the growth of the Head Start program, and the first comprehensive child care and family support legislation which was passed in 1990. Research and find out what roles Edward M. Kennedy and Hillary Rodham Clinton have had in the CDF.

Resources

Marian Wright Edelman by Joann J. Burch (The Millbrook Press, 1994)

Herstory: Women Who Changed the World, edited by Ruth Ashby and Deborah Gore Ohrn (Viking, 1995)

The Occupation of Wounded Knee

For many years Native Americans were ashamed of their heritage and faced discrimination and persecution. The civil rights movement of the 1960s inspired some of their leaders to fight for their rights. Here is their story.

The civil rights movement began in the United States during the 1950s, but it did not reach its peak until the sixties. By then, Americans of all ages, races, nationalities, and sexes were lobbying for equal rights. Ignored in all the protests and demonstrations, however, were the Native Americans. For years, this group had been discriminated against. Many still lived on Indian reservations where conditions were poor. They had other justifiable grievances, including limited opportunities and the lack of basic rights.

In 1968 the American Indian Movement was established, and Congress passed the Indian Civil Rights Act. This law guaranteed Indians the rights and privileges outlined in the Bill of Rights and recognized the legality of tribal law. It was a step in the right direction, but the Native Americans wanted more. Activists from several tribes banded together to present their grievances. When they were rebuffed, the group seized an abandoned federal prison on Alcatraz Island near San Francisco. For a year and a half they occupied the prison amidst a swirl of publicity. Their next seige was at Wounded Knee, South Dakota, the site of the 1890 massacre of the Sioux by the Seventh Cavalry. On February 28, 1973, members of the American Indian Movement, led by Dennis Banks and Russell Means, took over a trading post there.

Overall, these planned takeovers made non-Indians aware of the plight and grievances of Native Americans. As a result, some Native Americans began to take more pride in their heritage. But the most lasting effect was in the court actions which granted rights that had been in dispute for many years. For example, in 1971 the Aleuts and other native Alaskans won 40 million acres of land as well as nearly one billion dollars in settlements from the government. Despite receiving similar awards, several tribes still suffer from high unemployment and alcoholism rates.

Suggested Activities

Wealth In the 1980s and 1990s, gambling casinos cropped up on Indian reservations across the country. Find out what this meant to the welfare of the Native Americans and why it has raised controversy.

Discuss Why do you think Native American rights have been overlooked for so long?

Wounded Knee Wounded Knee, South Dakota, was the site of a previous Sioux massacre. Research events that led to that massacre.

Novel Idea Find some books or articles about the 1890 Wounded Knee incident written from the Native American point of view. Compare that version to what is printed in your school's history textbooks.

Adam Clayton Powell, Jr.

U.S. representative, minister, and civil rights leader are all titles that aptly describe Adam Clayton Powell, Jr. President Lyndon Johnson once called him one of the most powerful men in America. He was the first African American congressman to come from the East, serving as representative from the Harlem district in New York from 1945 to 1970. Powell also chaired the influential House Committee on Education and Labor and was instrumental in the establishment of the National Endowment for the Humanities.

Adam Clayton Powell, Jr.

Born in New Haven, Connecticut, in 1908, Powell was the son of Adam Clayton Powell, Sr., a minister and an author. Young Powell grew up in New York City and attended Colgate University in upstate New York. Following his education there, he attended Columbia University in 1932 and earned an M.A. degree. In addition to his studies, Powell assisted his father who was the minister of the Abyssinian Baptist Church in Harlem. During this time he decided to become a minister like his father. After attending Shaw University in Raleigh, North Carolina, for his doctor of divinity degree, Powell took over for his father at the Abyssinian church.

Like his father, Adam Powell, Jr., became an advocate for African American rights. He helped organize a buying-power movement which was a way to force white-owned businesses that depended on black customers to hire more black employees. Through picket lines, boycotts, and mass protests, some 10,000 new jobs were brought to Harlem. In 1941 he was elected to the New York City Council, and the following year he started publishing a weekly newspaper, *The People's Voice*.

This show of leadership and political activity helped Powell to win his first term as a U.S. representative in 1945. During the Kennedy and Johnson administrations, Powell was instrumental in obtaining federal aid for colleges and universities and legislated bills to fund teacher education and more libraries.

In the sixties Powell encountered some legal difficulties when he was accused of misusing public funds. As a result he was expelled from the House of Representatives, but the following month he was re-elected by the voters who disagreed with the expulsion. Powell served in Congress for a few more years until he was defeated in 1970. Only two short years after retiring, Powell died of cancer.

Suggested Activities

Expelled Another senator, Christopher Dodd, was also accused of misuse of funds, but he was allowed to keep his seat in Congress. Find out why Powell was expelled for the same alleged misuse.

Boycotts Discuss boycotts with the class and how they were effective in Powell's buying-power movement.

Resource Learn more about Powell's political life in the book *Adam Clayton Powell* by James S. Haskins (Africa World Press, Inc., 1992).

Hale House

Clara Hale was a widow with three children in 1932. She needed to work but wanted to be able to stay at home with her youngsters. A home day-care center proved to be the answer. In 1968 Hale retired but about a year later embarked on a new career when her daughter brought home a drug-addicted baby. Within a few short years, Hale House was founded to provide care for these infants.

Clara Hale

Clara McBride Hale was born in Philadelphia, Pennsylvania, in 1905. After her father died, her mother supported the family by cooking and renting out rooms in their home. Clara McBride attended school regularly and after graduating from high school married Thomas Hale. The young couple moved to Harlem in New York City where Thomas Hale had a floor-waxing business. Clara Hale worked nights cleaning theaters to help supplement their income. When her husband died in 1932, she was left with three young children to support. At first she continued her night job but added housecleaning jobs during the day. To be able to stay home with her children, Clara Hale began a day-care center and also took in foster children.

In 1968, one year after Clara McBride Hale retired, her daughter, Lorraine Hale, noticed a heroin addict who was falling asleep in the park with her infant falling out of her arms. Lorraine, who held a doctorate degree in child development, gave the young woman an address—her mother's—where the woman could get help. The following day, the woman showed up to surrender her baby while she got treatment for herself. Word spread quickly on the streets, and soon Clara Hale was caring for 22 drug-addicted babies.

At first, the venture was financed by Hale's three children who worked overtime to raise money to support it, but by the early seventies the city began to provide some funding. The Hales used the money to purchase and renovate a five-story home in Harlem. Hale House, as it was called, officially opened in 1975.

The only facility in the United States to treat the tiny victims of mothers who abused drugs, Hale House employed a social worker, a teacher, and a part-time staff of doctors and nurses. After the babies went through withdrawal and their mothers were healthy, they would be reunited. Hale's success rate was a phenomenal 97 percent, and less than one baby per year had to be put up for adoption.

When President Ronald Reagan cited Clara Hale's work in his 1985 State of the Union address before Congress, Hale House received national recognition and private funding. Today, the program has been expanded to help infants and mothers with AIDS. Lorraine Hale has continued her mother's work since Clara Hale's death in 1992.

Suggested Activity

Government Aid Discuss the role that the government should play in assisting programs such as Hale House. Would you be willing to work overtime to help support this cause?

Mikhail Baryshnikov

Mikhail Baryshnikov

When he was young, Mikhail Baryshnikov worried about his height because he was always the shortest boy in class. Eventually he learned to let go of his worries, and today he is regarded as one of the foremost ballet performers in the world.

Baryshnikov was destined to become a ballet dancer when he was born on January 27, 1948, in Riga, Latvia. His father was a military topographer in the Russian army, and his mother was a seamstress who loved ballet. It was she who encouraged Baryshnikov and enrolled him in ballet school. Although he was considered old for a beginning student (he was 12 years of age), he showed a great feeling for music. His body type was not ideal for ballet because he was not tall and slender, but he proved to be a talented student and was later admitted to the Vaganova Ballet School in Leningrad. There he studied under the famous ballet teacher Alexander Pushkin who treated Baryshnikov like a son. For the following three years he studied and practiced ballet for hours every day.

Upon graduation in 1966 Baryshnikov joined the Kirov Ballet Company. As a soloist for the dance troop, he gained international attention and won numerous awards. In 1968 a ballet was written especially for him by a famous Russian choreographer, as were all his later ballets. The Soviet government would not allow Baryshnikov to perform the work of other choreographers. While he was performing in Canada in 1974, Baryshnikov defected from the Soviet Union. He asked for political asylum in Canada, explaining that he had chosen to leave Russia for his artistic growth.

Later, he joined the American Ballet Theater in New York where he worked with another Soviet dancer, Natalia Makarova, who had also defected from Russia in the 1970s. Baryshnikov often collaborated with American choreographers, including the famous Twyla Tharp. In 1980 Baryshnikov became the American Ballet Theater's artistic director. In addition to dancing and choreographing, he launched a career in motion pictures and appeared in two films, *The Turning Point* (1976) and *White Nights* (1985).

Suggested Activities

Ballet Research and make a list of some of the basic ballet positions. Draw a picture to show how each step is executed. Try some of the positions yourself.

Roles What is the difference between the role of a male ballet dancer and the role of a female dancer?

Bravura Mikhail Baryshnikov employed a style of dancing known as *bravura*. Find out what is meant by this style and learn about other styles of ballet.

Actor, Writer, and Director

As a child he was a loner who spent little time with his sister and classmates. In his adult life he continued to be a loner in both his personal and stage personas. Who is this person? None other than comedian, writer, actor, director, and producer Woody Allen.

Woody Allen

Allen was born Allen Stewart Konigsberg in 1935 to Orthodox Jewish parents. His father, Martin, held a variety of short-lived jobs while his mother, Nettie, worked as an accountant in a flower shop. Allen disliked school despite the fact that he was considered bright. Only one subject seemed to interest him, and that was English composition. Allen avoided after-school activities and spent much time reading by himself. As a teenager he wrote and sent quips to newspaper gossip columnist Earl Wilson and earned money for one-liners he wrote for a press agent. After graduating from Midwood High School in Brooklyn, he briefly attended New York University and City College of New York. Low grades and poor attendance caused him to be expelled.

Allen found work as a writer for Sid Caesar's popular television weekly, *Your Show of Shows*, and then moved on to work for *The Garry Moore Show*. Despite receiving an excellent salary, Allen decided to leave the writing business to someone else and became a stand-up comedian. In his act, Allen portrayed himself as a hapless nerd who did not have any girlfriends. A breakthrough came when he was appearing in a New York nightclub. A film producer saw his act and offered him a job writing a screenplay for a movie. Although the film was a success, Allen did not like having so little say on how the project turned out. In the late 1960s, he wrote a screenplay for the first of many movies in which he would also star and direct. From *Take the Money and Run* (1969) to *Sleeper* (1973) to *Love and Death* (1975), Allen's audiences loved his sense of humor.

Another movie, *Annie Hall* (1977), made movie history when it swept the Oscar awards and won best picture, best director, best actress, and best original screenplay. A very funny look at male-female relationships, the movie starred Allen and Diane Keaton. Keaton's character introduced a whole new way for women to dress. The Annie Hall look, which featured tweed jackets worn over high collared shirts, a long scarf, and long skirts or baggy trousers, was soon adopted by women everywhere. Other films followed, but none has matched the success of *Annie Hall*, although many have been popular and award winning. Allen continues to live in New York City and can sometimes be seen playing clarinet with Dixieland bands at small pubs.

Suggested Activities

Plays In groups, write, direct, and act in a short play or skit about the problems of boy-girl relationships. Take turns presenting your plays.

One-Liners Woody Allen began his career by writing one-line jokes. Write new one-liners or share your favorite one-line jokes with the rest of the class.

Al Pacino

One of the blockbuster movie hits of the seventies was *The Godfather.* It won the Academy Award for best picture in 1972, and Al Pacino's brooding yet intelligent performance earned him an Oscar nomination for best supporting actor. Two years later the sequel, *The Godfather, Part II,* also won the best picture Oscar. In both films, Pacino played the continuing role of the good son in a Sicilian family.

Al Pacino

Al Pacino was born in New York in 1937. His father, a Sicilian-American, abandoned the family when Pacino was just two years old. After showing an early talent for acting, Pacino was admitted to New York's High School of Performing Arts. When he was 17 years old, however, he dropped out to break into the theater on his own. He supported himself with temporary jobs but continued to study and perfect his craft at Lee Strasberg's famous Actors Studio.

During the 1960s Pacino had some roles in off-Broadway productions. His performance in the play *The Indian Wants the Bronx* earned him an off-Broadway award or Obie. This success led to a starring role on Broadway the following year and a Tony Award for his work in the play *Does a Tiger Wear a Necklace?* After earning a small part in a 1969 film, Pacino played the lead in a low budget movie, *Panic in Needle Park.* Director Francis Ford Coppola noticed Pacino in the 1971 film and offered him the role of Michael Corleone in *The Godfather.* The film was a commercial and personal success for Pacino, who gained instant fame and accolades for his portrayal.

In the years that followed, Pacino enjoyed great success as an actor. His films in the seventies included *Serpico* (1973), *The Godfather, Part II* (1974), *Dog Day Afternoon* (1974), and *And Justice for All* (1977).

Pacino took on some controversial roles in the early eighties, and then was not seen in film for four years until he made the 1989 thriller *Sea of Love.* A cameo role in *Dick Tracy* and a leading part in *The Godfather, Part III* in the early nineties re-vitalized and re-established his career. In 1992 Pacino's portrayal of a blind man in *Scent of a Woman* earned him an Oscar, his first, for best actor. No matter what type of character he plays, Pacino brings an honesty and intensity to his role.

Suggested Activities

Discussion Why would an actor take on such diverse roles? Would it be easier to portray the same type of character from one movie to the next—romantic lead or action hero, for example?

Analogies Complete these analogies using the following words: Tony, Obie, Oscar, Emmy.

1. An ________ is to off–Broadway as a ________ is to Broadway.
2. A ________ is to Broadway as an ________ is to films.
3. An ________ is to film performances as an ________ is to television performances.

Sports Overview

On this page you will find an overview of sports during the seventies. See if you recognize any of the sports figures (the names have been bolded). Find out where they are today and if they are still active in their sport.

Auto Racing **Janet Guthrie** became the first woman to compete in the Indy 500. In 1978, her third try at Indy, she placed ninth.

Baseball On April 8, 1974, African American **Hank Aaron** broke Babe Ruth's lifetime home run record of 714.

Basketball Easily the biggest star in any sport was **Kareem Abdul Jabbar,** who stood 7 feet 2 inches (2.18 m) tall. A center, he collected six Most Valuable Player awards during his 20-year career.

Boxing Former Olympic champ **Muhammed Ali** won the world title a record three times—in 1964, 1974, and 1978.

Golf **Jack Nicklaus** dominated the golf scene during the 1970s.

Horse Racing **Robyn Smith** became the first woman to ride a horse to victory in a stakes race when she rode at New York's Aqueduct Track.

Steve Cauthen won thoroughbred racing's Triple Crown—the Kentucky Derby, Preakness, and Belmont Stakes in 1978. He was only 18 years old.

Jogging The sports craze of the seventies, jogging, was made popular by **Jim Fixx** who wrote a book about this kind of exercise. Out of this craze grew marathons which were races along roads over a distance of 26 miles (41.86 km).

Motorcycling Daredevil **Evel Knievel** planned to rocket 1,600 feet (485.33 m) across an Idaho canyon on a motorcycle. As the cycle streaked across the Snake River, a tail parachute opened too early. Knievel fell into the river and the motorcycle landed nose down on a rocky river bank. Luckily, Knievel suffered only superficial wounds.

Tennis Tennis superstars of the era included American **Jimmy Connors** and the Swedish **Bjorn Borg** who won Wimbledon a record five times between 1976 and 1980.

Bobby Riggs declared that no woman could beat a man in tennis, but **Billie Jean King** rose to the challenge and won the Battle of the Sexes in 1973.

Tracy Austin was the youngest ever United States Open champion at age 16. **Chris Evert,** famous for her two-handed backhand, won four United States Open tournaments from 1975 to 1978. To learn more about Evert, see page 47.

Suggested Activity

Sports Report Select one of the personalities discussed above and write a sports report about him or her. In your report include information about that person's childhood, any handicaps or obstacles he or she had to overcome, highlights of his or her career, and a description of some of his or her greatest accomplishments. Find and copy a picture of this sports figure, or draw one yourself, and attach it to your report.

Chris Evert

Chris Evert

Called the Ice Maiden by some, she had an outwardly calm demeanor that belied the fierce and competitive spirit underneath. Nothing seemed to distract her, and she impressed everyone with her accurate groundstrokes and unusual two-handed backhand. The athlete is, of course, Chris Evert.

Chris Evert was born on December 21, 1954, in Fort Lauderdale, Florida. The second of five children, she learned to play tennis from her father, Jimmy Evert, a one-time national junior tennis champion himself. Mr. Evert was also the manager and a teaching professional at the Holiday Park Tennis Center. The whole family spent time there and learned to play the game. At first, young Evert had problems holding the racket firmly with one hand, particularly on the backhand stroke, so the six-year-old took to using both hands. Most players considered the two-handed backhand unorthodox, but after Chris Evert began playing and winning tournaments, the two-hander became widely copied.

By the time she began entering junior tournaments, she was practicing several hours a day. That left her no time to attend parties or sleepovers with friends. She continued to do well in school and even graduated with honors from high school. By the time Evert was 14, she had already begun playing against top women players, and at age 15 she beat Australian Margaret Court, a high-ranking woman player. When Evert joined the tennis circuit the following year and arrived at the U.S. Open, she had already won 46 consecutive singles contests.

At age 18, Chris Evert turned professional. One of the biggest money winners in tennis at the time, she was the first woman to earn more than one million dollars. Another milestone was reached in 1974, when she won 35 consecutive titles by mid-year. She was also engaged to the top men's player, Jimmy Connors, but that union was broken off a few months later.

During her career, Chris Evert earned numerous tennis titles and awards, including being named the 1976 *Sports Illustrated* Sportswoman of the Year. She continued her number-one ranking until the rise of Martina Navratilova. The two alternately shared the number one spot until Evert retired.

In 1989 Evert left competitive tennis. Since then she has provided color commentary for televised tennis events. On a personal note, she is the mother of three sons. Although she enjoyed her tennis years, she claims that family is more important to her now.

Suggested Activities

Women's Role Find out what role Billie Jean King played in promoting women's tennis.

Rivals Evert and Martina Navratilova were fierce rivals on court. Find out more about Navratilova. Compare her style of play to Evert's.

Baseliner Chris Evert was a baseline player. What does that mean? What is the difference between a baseliner and a serve-and-volley player?

Seventies Sports Stars

There were many outstanding sports stars of the seventies including those found below. Read about each one and write the name of the athlete on the line provided. Use reference sources to help you with the answers.

1. ________________________ was the first Hispanic selected to the National Baseball Hall of Fame. As a player for the Pittsburgh Pirates he was named Most Valuable Player in the 1971 World Series. Tragically, he died in a plane crash in 1972.

2. ________________________ joined the Professional Bowlers Association in 1970 and in the following year set a record with 42 consecutive games of 200 or better. He was also the first bowler to win more than $1 million in prize money.

3. ________________________ was unbeatable in women's ice-skating in 1976. That year she won the United States and World championships plus an Olympic gold medal. She invented a new spin and her haircut, the wedge, was widely copied by girls everywhere.

4. ________________________ is known as The Golden Bear because of his blond hair and stocky build. A major force in golf during the seventies, he has won more major tournaments than any other golfer in history.

5. ________________________, a Canadian, joined the Boston Bruins when he was 18 years old. As a defenseman, he led his team to two Stanley Cup championships in 1970 and 1972. He was elected to the Hockey Hall of Fame in 1979.

6. ________________________ competed in the 1972 and 1976 Olympics. At the 1972 events she was 17 and just 4 feet 11 inches (1.5 m) tall. She was the first person to do a backflip on the balance beam, and she pioneered athletic movements in women's gymnastics.

7. ________________________ made history in 1976 when she became the first person from Liechtenstein to win a medal at the Winter Olympics. That year she won a bronze medal in the slalom. In the following Olympics she won three Alpine skiing medals.

8. ________________________, a fullback for the Miami Dolphins, led the team in 1972 to the only undefeated season inNatioal Football League history. After winning back-to-back Super Bowls in 1973 and 1974, he won the Most Valuable Player award in 1974.

9. ________________________ is credited with helping women's professional tennis grow. In 1973 she beat Bobby Riggs in the televised Battle of the Sexes. During her career she also won 12 Grand Slam singles titles. She helped found the Women's Tennis Association.

10. ________________________ was the first great runner to come from Africa. He trained in the mountains about 6,000 feet above sea level. His Olympic career spanned three games from 1964 to 1972. In 1965 he set world records in the 3,000 and 5,000 meter runs.

References

Awesome Athletes!, and T*he Everything You Want to Know About Sports Encyclopedia*, both Sports Illustrated for Kids Books, published by Bantam Books, 1995

Innovations of the 70s

The seventies decade was very productive in the field of science and technology. On this page you will find an overview of some of the most important innovations of the decade.

1970

- The first inexpensive (under $10) pocket calculators, developed by Clive Sinclair, are retailed in the United States.

1971

- The CAT (computerized axial tomography) scan, a tool for imaging the brain, is invented.
- The first commercial microprocessor is built. This invention makes it possible to build smaller, cheaper, and more efficient computers.
- Sociobiology is founded after Harvard biologist Edward O. Wilson studies the behavior of ants and other insects that live in groups.
- Lasers come into wide use to cut through metal, perform eye surgery, and create holograms.
- The first digital watches are manufactured.

1972

- The United States bans the use of the pesticide DDT when it is found to be harmful to plants, animals, and humans.
- *Pong*, the world's first commercial video game, is demonstrated.

1973

- *Skylab* is launched by the United States.

1974

- The Heimlich maneuver is developed by Cincinnati surgeon Henry Jay Heimlich to help save choking victims.
- UPCs (universal price codes) appear on food packages for use with scanners at checkout counters. They help speed up the process.

1975

- The world's first miniature television is produced.

1976

- The Concorde is the first civilian jet to break the sound barrier.
- On July 20, *Viking I* lands on Mars.
- CB's (citizen band radios) are the rage, and everyone from truckers to retirees uses them to communicate with one another.
- Scientists report that gases from spray cans can damage the ozone layer.

1977

- London to New York passenger service on the Concorde begins.
- MRI (magnetic resonance imaging) is first used in the medical industry.
- *Voyager* is launched.
- The first personal computer (Apple II) is manufactured.

1978

- The world's first test tube baby, Louise Joy Brown, is born in Great Britain.
- The Sony Walkman is introduced. It is the world's first personal stereo cassette player.

Suggested Activity

Importance Choose the most significant development from the list above. Explain your choice and how it has impacted your life today.

Skylab

On May 14, 1973, the United States launched *Skylab,* its first space station. Over the next nine months, three different flight crews were sent to live inside the orbiting spacecraft. Read on for more information about this historic space experiment.

Description *Skylab* was a space station in which people could work and live for extended periods of time. The main section of the craft contained a workshop where the crew lived. Inside the workshop were storage areas for food and water and crew quarters which contained individual sleeping compartments, toilets, a collapsible shower stall, exercise equipment, and a work area for experiments.

Equipment On the outside of *Skylab* were eight telescopes to study the sun, a shield to protect it from meteoroids, and six winglike solarcells to convert the sun's energy into electricity. Finally, a multiple docking adapter allowed rockets to connect to *Skylab.* Astronauts would then enter the craft through an air-lock module.

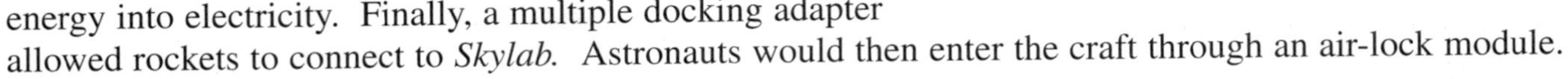

Crews Three different crews of three men each lived and worked on *Skylab* during a nine-month period. Each crew consisted of a commander, a science pilot (an expert on science experiments), and the pilot (an expert on space flight). The first crew spent 28 days in space; the second crew, 59 days; and the third crew, 84 days.

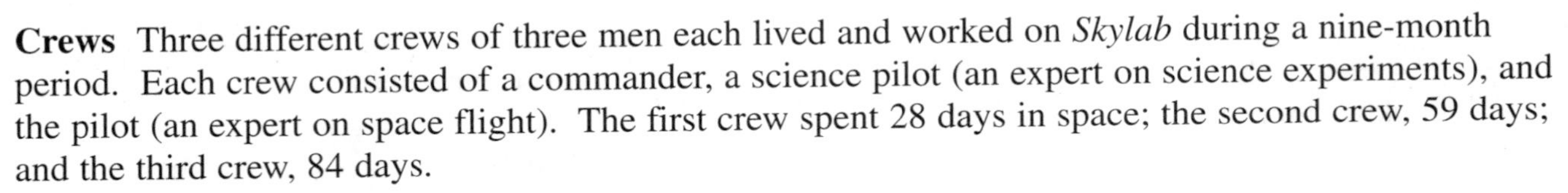

What Was Learned Over 160,000 pictures of the sun were taken during the three *Skylab* missions. Solar flares or eruptions were captured on film. Other photos showed much about the Earth's surface, including oil and mineral deposits and signs of air and water pollution. In addition, the crews recorded data about their own ability to adapt to a zero gravity environment and observed the behavior of minnows, spiders, and other small creatures in space.

End of Skylab After the third *Skylab* crew returned safely to Earth, *Skylab* continued to orbit the Earth for five more years. On July 12, 1979, it fell to Earth with some pieces landing in Australia and others plunging into the ocean.

Suggested Activity

Research In pairs or groups, research any of the following questions:

How did the astronauts reach *Skylab?*

What kinds of problems were encountered during the whole project?

What were the purposes of *Skylab,* and were they achieved?

How did the astronauts do everyday things like taking a shower and going to the bathroom?

What effect does the lack of exercise in space have on the body?

Pluto's Moon

While taking photographs at the Lowell Observatory in Arizona, astronomer Clyde Tombaugh discovered a new planet. The date was February 13, 1930. Since then, regular observations of the planet continued. Nothing new was discovered until 1978 when astronomer James W. Christy noticed a bulge on a photograph that he had taken of Pluto. As he scanned earlier photos of the planet, Christy noticed that the same bulge appeared in different spots. This exciting discovery was Pluto's moon, Charon.

Today, scientists know much more about Pluto and Charon than they did in the late seventies. Some amazing facts can be found below. Certain information is missing, though, and you will have to replace it. Complete the math problems in the box below and write the answers on the corresponding lines. Read the facts after all the blanks have been filled in.

1. 6,400 ÷ 800	4. 17,860 ÷ 47	7. 132.94 ÷ 46
2. 35,719 - 23,319	5. 10,148 - 6,552	8. 1,710 ÷ 95
3. 29.8 x 25	6. 99.830 + 147.850	

1. Earth is 80 times more massive than the moon, but Pluto is only________________times more massive than Charon.
2. Pluto and Charon are separated by only________________miles (19,950 km). That is just one-twentieth of the distance between the Earth and the moon.
3. The diameter of Charon is________________miles (1200 km), which is nearly one-half the diameter of Pluto.
4. Pluto and Charon are extremely cold with temperatures of________________degrees below zero Fahrenheit (-230 degrees Celsius).
5. Pluto's average distance from the sun is________________million miles (5,896 million kilometers).
6. It takes Pluto________________Earth years to make one orbit around the sun.
7. Pluto's average orbital speed is________________miles (4.74 km) per second.
8. While Earth rotates once every 24 hours, Pluto rotates once every 6 days, 9 hours,________________minutes.

Suggested Activity

Learn More Interested in learning more about this distant planet of Pluto? Choose one of the following activities to complete.

- Make a chart comparing facts about the Earth and its moon with Pluto and its moon, Charon.
- Find out why this statement is true: Pluto and Charon make up the closest thing to a double planet that we know of.
- How were the names Pluto and Charon chosen? What do the names represent?

Space Explorations

The United States launched a number of spacecraft during the seventies. Below you will find a brief introduction to each of these missions. After completing some research, add two or three more factual sentences to each description.

Apollo 13 You may already know about this flight from the 1990s movie of the same name. In 1970 this ill-fated mission was scheduled to land on the moon. Instead, an oxygen tank exploded, draining the air from the capsule. The astronauts were forced to move into the lunar module.

____

____

Mariner 9 In 1971, when *Mariner 9* orbited Mars, it became the first man-made object to orbit another planet.

____

____

Apollo 16* and *17 Both of these missions made trips to the moon.

____

____

Skylab Launched for a variety of experiments in space, *Skylab* was visited by three different crews during 1973 and 1974. The craft contained living quarters for the crew and was outfitted with solar equipment.

____

____

Mariner 10 This satellite transmitted detailed pictures of both Venus and Mercury back to Earth.

____

____

Viking I In 1976 this space probe landed on Mars. It sent back information about conditions on the planet, and it also searched for signs of life.

____

____

Voyager I On August 20, 1977, NASA launched the first of two *Voyager* spacecraft. *Voyager I* arrived at Jupiter in 1979 and discovered thin rings around the planet.

____

____

Voyager II Launched two weeks after *Voyager I*, it carried a 12-inch gold phonograph record containing greetings in dozens of Earth's languages.

____

____

Roots

In 1977 a new phenomenon was born: the television mini-series. Written by Alex Haley, the first mini-series, *Roots*, was the story of Haley's family, from its origins in Africa through the time of slavery to emancipation. More than three-fourths of the viewing population watched the televised eight-part series. In addition to being the first of its kind, *Roots* also was significant because of its realistic portrayal of African Americans. Most movie and television parts before that time portrayed blacks in a negative, stereotypical fashion.

Alex Haley

Alex Palmer Haley was born on August 11, 1921, in Ithaca, New York. His father, Simon Alexander Haley, was a professor and his mother, Bertha George Palmer Haley, was a teacher. Haley followed in their footsteps and attended Elizabeth City Teachers College for two years. After changing his mind about his choice of career, he joined the U.S. Coast Guard in which he served for 20 years.

When Haley left the Coast Guard in 1959 to become a freelance writer, he had been married to Nannie Branch for 18 years. Writing proved to be less than lucrative, and his already unstable financial situation put a strain on their relationship. By 1964, the marriage was over. That same year, Haley married Juliette Collins, but they also divorced.

Undeterred, Haley kept on writing and produced numerous articles but only two books. In 1965 he helped Malcolm X write his autobiography titled *The Autobiography of Malcolm X*. Eleven years later, Haley's book *Roots: The Saga of an American Family* gained him international fame. When the tale was produced as a television series, Haley acted as a consultant on the project. He also consulted on the television sequel, *Roots: The Next Generation*. Following the success of this program, he spent much of his time promoting and speaking about the novel. Although some critics wondered about the accuracy of his book, he was quick to point out that the events have a basis in actual history. Dialogue and characters' thoughts, however, were his creation.

Some time later, Haley was able to devote time to writing *My Search for Roots* in which he detailed the research involved in writing the original manuscript, but he never produced another novel. *Roots* had taken 12 years to research and write. In addition to being a bestseller, *Roots* earned Haley a Pulitzer prize and the NAACP's Spingarn Medal in 1977. Alex Haley died in 1992.

Suggested Activities

Video *Roots* may be available at your local video rental store or through your school district's media center. Watch selections in class and discuss the portrayal of African Americans at that time in history.

Mini *Roots* Write a mini-version of *Roots* about your own family heritage.

Judy Blume

Judy Blume

Beginning with the introduction of her book *Are You There God? It's Me, Margaret* in 1970, Judy Blume became a leading children's author. Her first book, *The One in the Middle Is the Green Kangaroo*, published in 1969, had already earned her respect in the children's literary world. Her work has sometimes caused concern or controversy, but Judy Blume still remains one of the most popular authors for children.

Judy Sussman Blume was born on February 12, 1938, in Elizabeth, New Jersey. Her father was Rudolph Sussman, a dentist, and her mother was Esther Rosenfeld Sussman. As a child Judy Sussman was an A student and did exactly as she was told, even though on the inside she wished she could rebel. She loved to read Nancy Drew mysteries, biographies, and horse stories but also longed to read about characters who shared problems that she and other young people were facing. She attended New York University, and the year before she graduated, in 1960, she married John W. Blume, an attorney. The couple had one daughter, Randy Lee, and a son, Laurence Andrew, but the marriage ended in divorce in 1975. Blume married George Cooper, a writer, in 1987.

Since her first book was published in 1969, Judy Blume has amassed awards from all over the United States, but her writing is not without controversy. Blume's direct, humorous style is part of her appeal, along with her ability to discuss openly and realistically subjects that are of concern to her readers. Sometimes her choice of themes and explicit treatment of mature issues have brought controversy. Some adults do not approve of Blume's use of frank language, and as a result some of her books have faced censorship by parents and librarians. Readers, on the other hand, are pleased to find an adult who seems to understand them and their real-life problems. Their fan letters relay this message over and over, and some even ask for the author's advice.

In addition to writing several juvenile fiction books, Judy Blume has authored young adult and adult books. *Wifey*, her first adult book, was published in 1978. That same year, an adaptation of her book *Forever* was made for television. Blume also contributed to the project *Free to Be You and Me* for the Ms. Foundation in 1974.

In recent years, Judy Blume founded KIDS Find and remains on the council of advisors for the National Coalition of Censorship.

Suggested Activities

Censorship Write the word *censorship* on the board. Discuss its meaning. Do you think adults have the right to censor what young people read? Debate whether Judy Blume's, or any author's, books should be censored.

Reading Read a Judy Blume book on your own or together in class. Identify the problems facing the main character. Discuss the problems and how they are resolved. Do you think these problems are believable? Have you experienced similar situations in your life?

An Olympic Artist

LeRoy Neiman

As a child LeRoy Neiman enjoyed drawing pictures, and when he was in the sixth grade, he won a national contest for his drawing of a whale. In high school, Neiman created posters for school activities and had a part-time job painting signs and windows for local stores. However, it was not until after he served in the Army during World War II, where he delighted his fellow GIs by painting murals on mess-hall walls, that Neiman considered art as a career.

After the war Neiman studied art in his hometown of St. Paul, Minnesota, and later at the Art Institute of Chicago. In Chicago he frequently attended sporting events, where he would draw or paint athletes, coaches, and competitions. He also became friendly with publisher Hugh Hefner and began to submit art to Hefner's new magazine, *Playboy*. For some 20 years Neiman traveled the world on assignment for the magazine, capturing scenes from sports and society in his own unique style.

In the 1970s Neiman gained even greater recognition as the official artist of the Olympic Games, and his work was featured on ABC Television's coverage of the events. He was named Olympic Artist of the Century. In 1978 and 1979 Neiman used a special electronic pen to capture the Super Bowl, allowing the viewing audience to see the work as it was being done.

Neiman's art has received both critical and popular acclaim. Although he may be best known for his works of celebrities and sports personalities, his personal goal is to explore all levels of society in his work. His subjects also include ordinary people, like beachgoers and bartenders. His unique blend of elements from several schools of art, including social realism, abstract expressionism, and abstract action painting, give his works life and capture the imagination. Bold lines, vibrant colors, and complex composition express feeling and action in a Neiman painting. On close examination, his images seem to be abstract shapes. Viewed from a distance, the shapes become dynamic figures that interact and move with great energy.

Suggested Activities

Compare LeRoy Neiman and Norman Rockwell both portrayed twentieth century American life in their paintings. Choose one work from each artist and compare and contrast the subject matter, technique, and style of the paintings. This may be done with the whole group, in small groups, pairs, or by yourself.

Prints In addition to original oil paintings, Neiman does eight serigraphs a year which are published as limited edition prints. Research the process for creating serigraphs, and write a set of directions for making a print. Discover answers to specific questions like the following: What is an artist's proof? How are prints numbered? What is a plate signed print? How does a print differ from a poster? Which prints are the most valuable? Invite an artist or other knowledgeable person to speak to your class about printmaking.

Christo

The seventies were filled with innovative art forms. One such form came from a conceptual artist known as Christo. He added a new dimension to the art world when he began to specialize in wrapping familiar objects such as flowers, magazines, and boxes. From these he progressed to monuments and eventually went on to envelop whole physical land areas such as in the *Running Fence* project (below). Because of their sizes, these creations are known as "earthworks."

Christo

Christo, whose full name is Christo Javacheff, was born and raised in Bulgaria in 1935, but he later became an American citizen. From 1952 to 1955 he attended the Academy of Art in Bulgaria and spent weekends in the country with groups of students whose job was to beautify the scenery. The students also showed farmers how to display their tractors to best advantage and encouraged them to cover haystacks with tarps. Possibly this early experience influenced Christo's later work as a wrap artist.

Christo begins his large projects with sketches. He then does the actual construction work. He films and photographs the work before unwrapping the entire project. By selling these films and photos, Christo raises money for his next project. Through his work, Christo seeks to lead people to see familiar scenes in a new way and to show the susceptibility of society to packaging. Despite the transitory nature of his work, Christo remains one of the most popular artists in the world.

Christo's *Running Fence* project was begun in 1972 and was finally completed September 10, 1976. The fence extended east and west near Freeway 101, north of San Francisco, on the private properties of 59 ranchers. Carefully planned, it ran through two counties, crossing 14 towns and allowing passage for cars and cattle. 18 feet (5.4 m) high and 24.5 miles (38.4 km) long, *Running Fence* consisted of 165,000 yards of heavy, white nylon fabric hung from a steel cable and strung between 2,050 steel poles. Two weeks after the sculpture's completion, it was removed. All of its materials were then given to the ranchers.

Suggested Activities

Wrap Brainstorm a list of materials to use for wrapping other items, such as newspapers, plastic bags, aluminum foil, and so forth. Use any material of your choice to wrap a common classroom object (book, clock, chair, etc.). Display all wrapped objects for one or two days before removing the wrapping materials.

Research Research other artistic innovations and popular expressions of the seventies. Two possibilities are graffiti art and album cover art. Find out about the history of the art styles and bring in examples.

The Many Faces of Rock

Rock music continued to evolve and change in the seventies, and a number of new musical forms were popular. Read about some of the prominent musical styles and musicians of the seventies. Research further any individual or group that especially interests you.

Glam Rock Rock artists donned makeup and outrageous clothing such as foil-like suits, glitter, and stacked heels. David Bowie is perhaps the best known in this category. He even adopted different characters, the most famous of which is Ziggy Stardust. Queen and Elton John were also prominent glam rockers.

Punk Punk music began in New York City and was exported to Britain by a clothing store manager. Cut up jeans and T-shirts, harsh makeup, safety-pin jewelry, and spiked and dyed hair completed the look. Blondie was a notable punk group.

Disco A shortened form of *discotheque*, a French term for a night club that features dancing, this dance music craze had been growing in New York City for some time as a social outlet. It did not become mainstream until the 1978 movie *Saturday Night Fever* brought it to national attention. The Bee Gees sang many of the hits from the movie track, but singer Donna Summer was the undisputed queen of disco.

Reggae A combination of rock, rhythm and blues, and Jamaican music, reggae is distinctive with its lilting, off-beat style. Popularized by Bob Marley, the reggae style was successfully adapted by other groups such as The Clash and The Police.

Rock Opera In 1975, the rock opera album *Tommy* by The Who was made into a film. Elton John and Tina Turner starred as did two members of the band, Roger Daltrey and Keith Moon. Another popular rock opera of the seventies was *Jesus Christ Superstar*.

The following is a list of some other favorite seventies artists and their songs.

Simon and Garfunkel sang "Bridge Over Troubled Water" which became the first big hit of 1970.

Marvin Gaye's 1971 album *What's Going On*? was a social commentary on Vietnam, pollution, and the world in which we live.

Janis Joplin's single "Me and Bobby McGee" became a posthumous hit in 1971.

Carole King had a laid-back, soft-rock approach. Her album *Tapestry* sold 13 million copies.

Stevie Wonder continued to touch upon social matters with his *Innervisions* album.

Pink Floyd focused on the dark side of life with its *Dark Side of the Moon* album.

Bruce Springsteen was the authentic blue-collar rock hero with his *Born to Run* album.

Peter Frampton came alive with songs like "Do You Feel Like We Do?" and "Show Me the Way."

Fleetwood Mac had the top album, *Rumours,* in the United States and Britain in 1977.

Electric Light Orchestra (ELO) was a space-age smash with its *Out of the Blue* album.

Blondie took a disco approach with *Heart of Glass*.

Osmonds vs. Jacksons

Music was a family affair for both the Osmonds and the Jacksons, who were popular during the seventies. Although they had different backgrounds and musical styles, they were alike in many ways. Compare and contrast the Osmonds with the Jacksons by writing the information from the list below in the correct section of the chart.

- Mormon
- five brothers
- signed with Motown
- first single was "One Bad Apple"
- sisters Janet and LaToya were also singers
- choreographed their dancing
- appeared regularly on TV
- Alan, Wayne, Merrill, Jay, Donny
- first single was "I Want You Back"
- switched to country music
- African American
- all vocals
- Jackie, Tito, Jermaine, Marlon, Michael
- sister Marie was also a singer
- youngest member of the group was the most popular

Osmonds	
Both	
Jacksons	

Linda Ronstadt

She started out as a rock and roll musician but won her first Grammy for singing a country tune. In the years to follow she experimented with standards, musicals, and folk music from her Mexican heritage. Linda Ronstadt's faithful fans never know quite what to expect from her.

Linda Ronstadt

Linda Ronstadt was born on July 15, 1946, in Tucson, Arizona. She was the third child in a family of two boys and two girls. Her father, Gilbert, an accomplished musician, ran his father's business. Her mother, Ruthmary Copeman, was a member of a prominent Michigan family, who first met her husband while she was attending an Arizona college.

As a child Linda Ronstadt was introduced to Mexican folk music by her father. She also loved to listen to music on the radio, especially the country tunes of Hank Williams. In her early teens, she and her sister and older brother formed a singing group. They played small gigs in and around Tucson. After high school Ronstadt left for Los Angeles to become a professional singer on her own. The Stone Poneys was her first group, but after a series of minor successes they broke up. However, Ronstadt's voice had not gone unnoticed. A problem of ever-changing backup bands hindered her work, as did her dependence on producers to shape her sound, but when Ronstadt found Peter Asher she finally felt comfortable musically and was able to obtain the elusive commercial and critical success that she longed for. Her 1974 album *Heart Like a Wheel* put her on the charts. Out of this platinum album came her first Grammy for Best Female Country Vocal for her rendition of the Hank Williams' tune "I Can't Help It." A 1976 album, *Hasten Down the Wind*, earned her a second Grammy. The following year Ronstadt changed musical direction again when she took the advice of the Rolling Stones' singer Mick Jagger to try harder rock. The result was her version of the Stones' "Tumbling Dice" on the platinum winning album *Simple Dreams*.

In the years that followed, Ronstadt departed from rock and roll by performing in the Gilbert and Sullivan musical *Pirates of Penzance*. During the 1980s she revamped her style even more and performed standard pop and jazz tunes with Nelson Riddle's big band and recorded a country album with Dolly Parton and Emmylou Harris. Most recently, Linda Ronstadt has returned to the folk music she learned during her childhood.

Suggested Activities

Listening Compare Linda Ronstadt's version of a song with that of the original artist. Explore the differences she contributes to the new versions.

Currently Ronstadt won a Grammy for Best Performance by a Mexican American. Learn more about the album that earned her this award.

Making Life Easier

Throughout the 1970s, a number of new items made their way to the supermarket shelves. Today these things are common to most households. Read each description below. Mark an X next to each item described that you or someone in your home uses today.

Maybelline Nail Color Maybelline cosmetics had been around since 1917, when it first introduced mascara, eye shadow, and eye pencils. In 1973 the company branched out into lip and nail products, including nail polish. Today Maybelline is the second largest cosmetic company in the United States.

Bounce This fabric softener was different because it came in sheets that were placed into the dryer along with a load of clothes. Invented in 1972, Bounce fabric softener sheets are now available in a variety of fragrances.

L'eggs The 1970 introduction of these pantyhose established two marketing firsts : They were packaged in plastic eggs, and they could be found in supermarkets and convenience stores. These days, the eggs have been replaced by cardboard containers, but L'eggs remain the best selling pantyhose in America.

Tidy Cat Ed Lowe had already been selling kitty litter to pet stores when he persuaded grocery stores to stock his product. He changed the name to Tidy Cat, and today it is the best selling cat-box filler in the United States.

Mr. Coffee Filters Inventor Vince Marotta was in search of a better way to make coffee when he observed restaurants using a white cloth in their percolators. Marotta used a paper filter in his coffeemaker, and today more than 10 billion Mr. Coffee filters are sold each year.

Ziploc Storage Bags The Dow Chemical Company manufactured a number of new consumer products during the 50s and 60s, including Saran Wrap, Handi-Wrap, and Dow Oven Cleaner. Ziploc Storage Bags debuted in 1970 and are unique because of their watertight, zipper-like seal.

Clairol Herbal Essence Commercial shampoos had been around since the 1880s, but in 1971 Clairol invented a shampoo with herbal fragrance. The product was designed to target the back-to-nature movement embraced by many young people in the early 70s.

Choose one of the products described above. In the space below, write at least five different uses for that product other than its intended use.

____

____

____

____

____

Seventies Inventions

On this page you can read about some inventors and the new ideas they formulated in the seventies. Research and write a one-page report about the invention that interests you most. Explain why you chose it and what lasting benefits it has brought to mankind.

Microprocessor In 1971 three Intel Corporation engineers built the first commercial microprocessor. This tiny, integrated circuit, or microchip, contained a computer processor which was the basis for the computer revolution of the 80s and 90s.

Food Processor Built in the same year as the microprocessor, the food processor was a new and versatile kitchen tool. It was invented by Frenchman Pierre Verdon and could be used to mix, chop, or slice food.

Home Video Game In 1972 Ralph Baer invented the world's first home video game. This simulated table tennis game was called *Odyssey* and was played with a special console that was hooked up to a regular television screen. Two knobs on the console controlled the up and down movements of the paddles. Later that year, Atari released the first coin-operated video game called *Pong*. Developed by computer pioneer Nolan Bushnell, the game was an electronic version of ping-pong. In the late seventies some video games began to use vector graphics, and a whole series of *Pac Man* games became popular.

CAT Scanner X-rays had traditionally been used to view dense parts of the body, particularly the bones, but it provided poor pictures of the soft tissue in the brain. In 1972 British researcher Godfrey Hounsfield developed the CAT (computerized axial tomography) scanner to get a better look inside the brain. The scanner took thousands of X-ray pictures before spending hours analyzing them. Images were then displayed on a screen so doctors could see the brain from a number of different angles.

MRI Scanner Five years after the CAT scanner was invented in 1972, the MRI scanner was developed. MRI, or magnetic resonance imaging, allowed doctors to look inside a person's body without using harmful X-rays. In 1984 the Food and Drug Administration gave final approval for the sale and use of the MRI scanner.

Personal Computer The Altair 8800 was the first commercial personal computer, but it came in kit form and lacked a keyboard and screen. Two California college dropouts, Steven Jobs and Stephen Wozniak, created and marketed the first truly useful personal computer in 1976 and called it the Apple.

Skylab In 1973 the United States launched an unmanned space station in orbit. During the next nine months, three different crews visited the craft. For additional information about *Skylab* see page 50.

The Seventies Wardrobe

Fashions for Women

A wide variety of clothing styles evolved during the seventies. At the beginning of the decade, jeans and the unisex look were popular, but the 1978 movie *Annie Hall* spawned a new look, as did the disco craze. Even the back-to-earth movement influenced fashions with the peasant look.

On this and the next page you can see some of the most popular styles during this time period.

Farrah Fawcett bangs,
hot pants, and
platform shoes

Annie Hall
Granny dresses and boots

The Seventies Wardrobe *(cont.)*

Fashions for Men 1970s

Men's fashions were also influenced by the jogging craze, punk music, and a growing interest in black cultural identity.

rooster cuts,
dyed hair, slashed T-shirts and jeans

gold chains,
open neck shirt,
bellbottoms, and
neat, clean cuts with long sideburns

Elsewhere . . .

1970

- Charles DeGaulle dies.
- Salvador Allende, a Marxist, is elected president of Chile.
- Cyclones and floods kill 500,000 in East Pakistan.
- Thirty thousand die in Peru due to earthquakes, floods, and landslides.
- Five planes are hijacked by Black September Palestinian guerillas.
- The United States invades Cambodia.
- Civil war erupts in Jordan.

1971

- SALT agreement is reached at Moscow Summit.
- People's Republic of China enters the UN.
- War breaks out between India and Pakistan.
- The nation of Bangladesh is created.
- In Switzerland, women are granted the right to vote.
- Fighting in Indochina spreads to Laos and Cambodia.
- Three Russian cosmonauts die when their *Soyuz 11* capsule develops a leak on re-entry into the Earth's atmosphere.

1972

- The Berlin Wall is opened to allow family visits.
- Israeli athletes are murdered at the Munich Olympics.
- The U.S.S.R. agrees to purchase $750 million worth of U.S. surplus grain.
- Ceylon becomes a republic and changes its name to Sri Lanka.
- Philippine leader Ferdinand Marcos declares martial law.
- Okinawa is returned to Japan.
- Bangladesh is established as a sovereign state.
- The U.S.S.R. wins 50 gold medals at the Summer Olympics in Munich.
- A 47 day coal strike cripples Great Britain.

1973

- Vietnam declares a cease-fire.
- A military coup occurs in Chile.
- The Yom Kippur Arab-Israeli War takes place.
- Arabs raise oil prices and impose an oil embargo on the United States.
- Mid-East peace talks open in Geneva.
- The Bahamas are granted their independence from British rule.
- Spanish premier Luis Carrero Blanco is assassinated.

1974

- Grenada, a former British colony, declares its independence.
- Ethiopian emperor Haile Selassie is deposed.
- India explodes its first atomic bomb.
- Civil war breaks out in Cyprus.
- Russian writer Alexander Solzhenitsyn goes into exile.
- Golda Meir steps down.
- Yitzhak Rabin is named to head the Israeli cabinet.
- British Prime Minister Edward Heath resigns and is succeeded by Harold Wilson.
- U.S. Secretary of State Henry Kissinger negotiates a cease-fire on the Golan Heights.
- In Argentina, Juan Perón dies and is succeeded by his wife, Isabel.
- Two Arab countries lift the oil embargo against the United States.

1975

- Papua, New Guinea, and Surinam gain their independence.
- Communists take over Cambodia and South Vietnam.
- Egypt reopens the Suez Canal.
- Saigon falls in Vietnam.
- Mozambique and Angola become independent.
- Former Ethiopian emperor Haile Selassie dies.
- The International Women's Year is proclaimed.
- The Helsinki Agreement is signed.
- King Faisal of Saudi Arabia is assassinated by a nephew who is punished by beheading.
- A Japanese woman becomes the first female to climb Mt. Everest.

Elsewhere . . . (cont.)

1976

- Rioting takes place in Soweto, South Africa.
- Civil war breaks out in Angola.
- Former chairman of China, Mao Tse-tung, dies.
- The Concorde makes its first transatlantic flight.
- The president of Argentina is overthrown.
- The Summer Olympics are held in Montreal, Canada; the Winter Olympics are held in Innsbruck, Austria.
- Great Britain introduces high-speed trains.
- North and South Vietnam are united.
- In Nicaragua civil war breaks out.

1977

- Steve Biko, black trade union leader, dies in police custody in South Africa.
- Egypt's leader Anwar Sadat makes an historic trip to Israel on November 19.
- Indira Gandhi resigns as prime minister of India.
- Israeli Prime Minister Yitzhak Rabin resigns and is succeeded by Menachem Begin.
- The Pakistan army overthrows the government and General Zia comes to power.
- French is adopted as the official language of Quebec.
- Great Britain celebrates the Silver Jubilee of Queen Elizabeth II.
- London to New York passenger service on the Concorde begins.

1978

- In England, the first test-tube baby is born.
- More than 900 Americans commit suicide in Jim Jones's People's Temple in Guyana, South America.
- Violence sweeps Nicaragua as Sandanista guerillas attempt to overthrow the government.
- A military junta seizes power in Afghanistan.
- The Nobel Peace Prize is awarded to Israeli Premier Menachem Begin and Egyptian President Anwar Sadat.
- Earthquakes hit Greece, Japan, Mexico, Iran, and central Europe.
- Former Italian prime minister Aldo Moro is murdered.
- John Paul II becomes the first Polish pope.
- A massive oil spill occurs along the coast of France when the tanker *Amoco Cadiz* wrecks.

1979

- Maria Pintassilgo becomes Portugal's first female prime minister.
- The Shah of Iran abdicates.
- Ayatollah Khomeini returns from exile.
- Iran becomes the Islamic Republic of Iran.
- Hostages are seized as students occupy the American embassy in Tehran.
- The Vietnamese depose the Pol Pot regime in Cambodia.
- Russia invades Afghanistan.
- The Camp David Accord leads to an Egypt-Israel peace treaty.
- Idi Amin, president of Uganda, is overthrown.
- Mother Teresa wins the Nobel Peace Prize.
- The SALT 2 arms treaty is signed but withdrawn after Soviet troops invade Afghanistan.
- Rhodesian peace talks lead to promise of an independent Zimbabwe.
- Margaret Thatcher becomes prime minister in Britain.
- War is fought between China and Vietnam.
- The United States and China establish diplomatic relations.
- General Anastasio Somoza of Nicaragua is overthrown.

Olympic Highlights

Some of the most notable Olympic games ever were held during the 1970s. Records were set, perfect scores were earned, and terrorist activity marred one summer Olympics. Research the Olympics of the seventies decade and fill in the blanks with the names of the correct athletes.

1972 Summer Olympics, Munich, West Germany

1. A 22-year-old American swimmer,____________________, won an unprecedented seven gold medals.
2. For the first time since 1908, the marathon was won by an American,____________________.
3. Soviet____________________introduced a more acrobatic style to gymastics.
4. Australian swimmer____________________won five medals here and became the only woman to win three individual gold medals in world record time.
5. ____________________of Kenya won two gold and two silver medals in his races at the 1968 and 1972 Olympics.
6. American swimmer____________________was stripped of his gold medal after it was learned he took a drug for his asthma condition before competing.

1972 Winter Olympics, Sapporo, Japan

7. ____________________, an American figure skater, skated gracefully to win the women's gold medal.
8. Austrian skier____________________was disqualified from the games because of alleged violations of the amateur code.

1976 Summer Olympics, Montreal, Canada

9. 14-year-old Romanian____________________became the first gymnast to earn a perfect 10.
10. American____________________won the gold in the grueling decathlon event.
11. A protege of former Olympian Dr. Sammy Lee,____________________won a silver medal in platform diving.
12. Cuban____________________won an unprecedented double gold in the 400- and 800-meter events.
13. American boxers struck gold, including Michael Spinks, Leon Spinks, and light welterweight____________________.

1976 Winter Olympics, Innsbruck, Austria

14. ____________________, a speedskater from Detroit, won a gold, a silver, and a bronze medal.
15. Austrian skier____________________came from behind to win the gold medal in the downhill.
16. Russian pairs skaters Aleksandr Zaitsev and____________________captured the hearts of many, as well as the gold medal.

Passages

Births

1970

- Ricky Shroeder and River Phoenix, actors
- Andre Agassi, tennis superstar

1973

- Tempestt Bledsoe, actress

1975

- Drew Barrymore, actress and granddaughter of John Barrymore

1976

- Jennifer Capriati, tennis star

Deaths

1970

- Gypsy Rose Lee, entertainer and stripper
- Charles De Gaulle, France's leader
- Erle Stanley Gardner, creator of *Perry Mason*

1971

- Jim Morrison of The Doors
- Louis Armstrong, African American jazz musician
- Audie Murphy, World War I hero
- Coco Chanel, French fashion designer

1972

- Harry S. Truman, former U.S. president
- Mahalia Jackson, African American gospel singer
- J. Edgar Hoover, FBI director since 1924
- Jackie Robinson, first African American to play major league baseball
- Roberto Clemente, baseball great

1973

- Lyndon B. Johnson, former U.S. president
- Pearl S. Buck, winner of Nobel Prize for Literature
- Pablo Picasso, French painter
- Pablo Casals, Spanish cellist
- David Ben-Gurion, Israeli founder and former premier
- Betty Grable, actress and WWII pin-up girl

1974

- Charles Lindbergh, aviation pioneer
- Jack Benny, American actor and comedian
- Samuel Goldwyn, pioneer Hollywood producer

1975

- Chiang Kai-shek, president of Nationalist China
- Emperor Haile Selassie of Ethiopia
- Josephine Baker, African American singer and dancer

1976

- Agatha Christie, mystery novelist
- Guy Lombardo, big-band leader
- Howard Hughes and J. Paul Getty, both American billionaires
- Mao Tse-tung, leader of People's Republic of China
- Alexander Calder, American sculptor

1977

- Elvis Presley, the king of rock and roll
- Groucho Marx, actor and comedian
- Maria Callas, Greek American operatic singer
- Erroll Garner, jazz pianist
- James Jones, American novelist

1978

- Hubert Humphrey, former U.S. vice president
- Margaret Mead, American anthropologist
- Golda Meir, former prime minister of Israel
- Norman Rockwell, illustrator and painter of Americana

1979

- Nelson Rockefeller, former U.S. vice president
- Emmett Kelly, famous American clown
- Jack Haley, the Tin Man in *The Wizard of Oz*
- Lester Flatt, country singer

The Aswan High Dam

Every year in Egypt the Nile River flooded. This water was necessary for growing crops, but often there was too much. From July to October the water level could rise up to 25 feet (8 m) above what it was in May. Today, there is no more fluctuation of water levels thanks to the Aswan High Dam which was built in 1971.

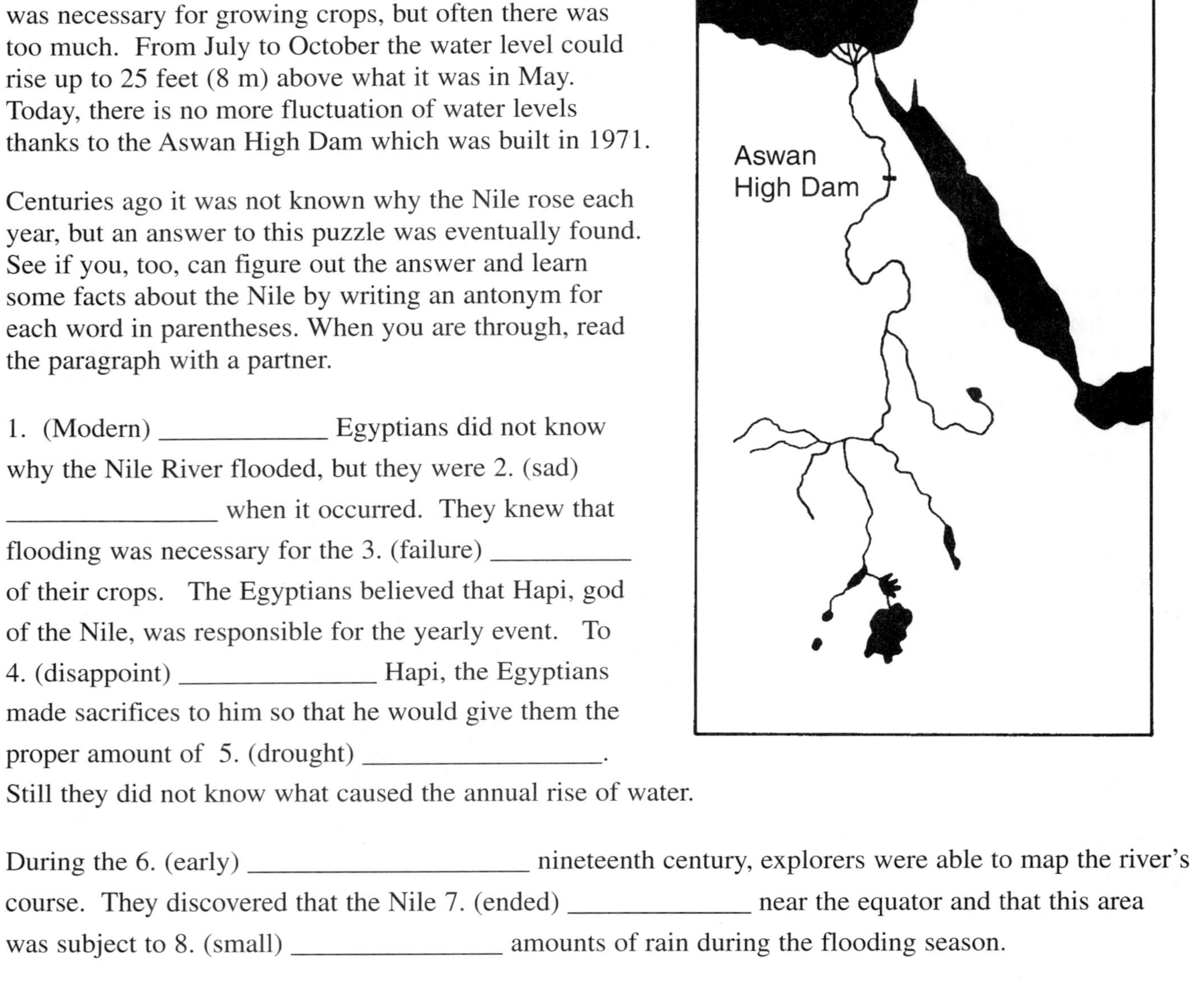

Centuries ago it was not known why the Nile rose each year, but an answer to this puzzle was eventually found. See if you, too, can figure out the answer and learn some facts about the Nile by writing an antonym for each word in parentheses. When you are through, read the paragraph with a partner.

1. (Modern) ____________ Egyptians did not know why the Nile River flooded, but they were 2. (sad) _______________ when it occurred. They knew that flooding was necessary for the 3. (failure) __________ of their crops. The Egyptians believed that Hapi, god of the Nile, was responsible for the yearly event. To 4. (disappoint) ______________ Hapi, the Egyptians made sacrifices to him so that he would give them the proper amount of 5. (drought) _________________. Still they did not know what caused the annual rise of water.

During the 6. (early) ____________________ nineteenth century, explorers were able to map the river's course. They discovered that the Nile 7. (ended) _____________ near the equator and that this area was subject to 8. (small) _______________ amounts of rain during the flooding season.

The riddle of the Nile was finally solved. Today the Nile, which is the 9. (shortest) ____________ river in the world, no longer floods. The Aswan High Dam, which was built in 1971, 10. (permits) ________ the river from overflowing.

Answers (Fold under before copying.) These are suggested answers. Accept any others that are appropriate.

1. ancient, old 2. happy 3. success 4. please, satisfy 5 flooding, rain 6. late 7. started, began 8. large, great
9. longest 10. prevents, stops

Independence for African Nations

Throughout the seventies, the process of decolonization in Africa continued at a brisk pace. Great Britain, France, Portugal, Belgium, Spain, and Italy were all pressured to relinquish their claims to the continent. Within a 30-year period beginning in the 1950s, 50 new states were created there. South Africa, however, remained the same and continued its apartheid policy.

On the map below, match the number of the country to its name in the list. Also supply the name of the country from which it received its independence and the year in which it was granted.

Djibouti ______________________________

Guinea Bissau ______________________________

Mozambique ______________________________

Comoros Islands ______________________________

Angola ______________________________

West Sahara ______________________________

Answers (Fold under before copying.)

Djibouti: 2, France, 1977—Guinea Bissau: 6, Portugal, 1974—Mozambique: 3, Portugal, 1975—Comoros Islands: 1, Portugal, 1975—Angola: 4, Portugal, 1975—West Sahara: 5, Spain—1975

Pierre Trudeau

Pierre Trudeau

Canadian Prime Minister Pierre Trudeau has the distinction of serving longer than any other contemporary leader in the modern Western world. From 1968 to 1984 he guided his country through some of its most tumultuous times. He was quite popular with the Canadian people.

Pierre Trudeau was born on October 18, 1919, in Montreal, Canada. His father was a lawyer who also owned a chain of service stations. When the elder Trudeau died in 1935, he left his family a five-million dollar fortune. Young Trudeau graduated from the University of Montreal Law School in 1943 and continued with his education at Harvard University in the United States, the University of Paris, and the London School of Economics. For a while, Trudeau traveled through Eastern Europe to China during its 1949 revolution. He also visited Vietnam and Cambodia while they were fighting the French. These actions earned him the reputation of being a radical and prevented him, at first, from obtaining a teaching position at the University of Montreal. Later, in 1961, Trudeau did earn a teaching post there but left in 1965 to join the Liberal party. That same year he was elected to the House of Commons and successfully argued against the French-speaking separatists who were lobbying for the secession of Quebec. He was appointed minister of justice and attorney general of Canada in 1967. During his brief term, he worked to expand social welfare programs and liberalize laws pertaining to areas such as divorce and gambling. Following Prime Minister Lester Pearson's retirement in 1968, Trudeau was selected as his replacement.

Trudeau's main cause was a just society in which he reorganized various governmental departments and introduced laws to guarantee the rights of the French-speaking minority, as well as native Canadians. His administration also helped pass the Official Languages Act which recognized English and French as Canada's two official languages.

One of his policies was not so popular, however. The American government was displeased when he avoided entering into military alliances and sought, instead, to keep Canada neutral in international affairs. The 1970s provided Trudeau with his biggest challenge when the country suffered increasing unemployment, inflation, and labor unrest. Throughout the decade, his Liberal party began to lose support. When French-speaking separatists in Quebec began to employ terrorist tactics, Trudeau was forced to declare a national emergency. In 1984 Trudeau resigned and was succeeded by Liberal John Turner. A charismatic leader, Trudean returned to practicing law after he left office.

Suggested Activity

Debate Debate the topic of Quebec and whether or not the province should be allowed to be an independent country.

The Great Lakes

North America is marked by five huge lakes bordered by Canada to the North and the United States of America to the south. Known as the Great Lakes, they are an important link between the two neighboring countries. A series of locks and canals have been built through the lakes to allow ships to sail to the oceans. Over the years increased industrialization caused the lakes to become polluted. Many of the lakes' fish died, and beaches were closed to the public. In 1972 the United States and Canada signed a mutual agreement to clean up the pollution in the Great Lakes.

Learn more about the Great Lakes region with the quiz below. Fill in the blanks in the following sentences. When you are through, check your answers using an atlas or a map of the Great Lakes region.

1. The United States and Canadian border runs across the center of these four lakes: __________, __________, __________, and __________.
2. The largest of the five lakes is __________.
3. The Great Lakes are linked to the Atlantic Ocean by the __________.
4. Toronto borders on Lake __________.
5. Niagara Falls lies between these two lakes: __________ and __________.
6. Wisconsin borders two great lakes, __________ and __________.
7. Cleveland lies on Lake __________.
8. Many locks and canals have been built throughout the Great Lakes so that ships can sail from Lake __________ to the oceans.
9. New York state borders these two lakes: __________ and __________.
10. The smallest of the five lakes is __________.
11. Lake Huron forms a border of this state: __________.
12. The state of Ohio borders on this lake: __________.
13. Chicago lies on this lake: __________.
14. Lake Erie forms a border of these four states: __________, __________, __________, and __________.

Answers (Fold under before copying.)

1\. Erie, Ontario, Huron, and Superior 2. Lake Superior 3. St. Lawrence River 4. Ontario 5. Lake Ontario, Lake Erie 6. Superior, Michigan 7. Erie 8. Superior 9. Erie, Ontario 10. Ontario 11. Michigan 12. Erie 13. Michigan 14. Michigan, Ohio, Pennsylvania, New York

The Amazon Rain Forest

In 1971 construction began in Brazil for a major trans-Amazon highway to open up remote areas of the rain forest for settlement and development. Huge areas of the Amazon rain forest were cut down and burned to make way for about one million new settlers. Because the large cities were so overcrowded and most people were unable to find work there, the government offered lucrative incentives to families who moved to the Amazon. Each family would be given a 240-acre piece of land, housing, and a small salary for a few months. Plans were made to build schools, health facilities, and other services. Thousands made the move but had to give up after only a few months because life in the rain forest was so difficult. The project was deemed a failure.

Not only was the project a failure, but it led to the destruction of a great deal of the Amazon rain forest. The result of this devastation was that much of the rain forest habitat was lost forever, and the soil eroded and turned into poor agricultural land. This is indeed a tragedy because the rain forest is so important to the ecology of not only the Amazon but of the world.

Listed below are some ways in which the rain forest is important to mankind. Choose and circle the best response in each parentheses.

1. The rain forest provides (protection/habitats) for many species of plants and animals.
2. When their habitats are destroyed, these organisms no longer have a (function/home), and the whole species is in danger of dying off.
3. More than (200,000/500) different Indian tribes live in the Amazon rain forest.
4. Their (existence/instinct), however, is threatened by the destruction of the land which is their home.
5. Everything that they need—clothing, food, shelter, medicine—can be provided by (resources/animals) found in the rain forest.
6. Western civilization is dependent on the Amazon rain forest as its source of new (medicines/wood).
7. As more and more land is destroyed, many medicinal plants will become (extinct/expensive).
8. Another concern for the Amazon environment is (global warming/fossil fuels).
9. Fossil fuels produce (carbon dioxide/carbon monoxide) emissions.
10. Trees are necessary to take in this carbon dioxide and release (oxygen/hydrogen) which is so important to human and animal life.
11. In addition, huge areas of trees like those in the rain forest are important to the (rainfall/water cycle).
12. All of the (grassland/tropical climate) depends on the success of the water cycle.

Answers (Fold under before copying.)

1. habitats 2. home 3. 500 4. existence 5. resources 6. medicines 7. extinct 8. fossil fuels 9. carbon dioxide 10. oxygen 11. water cycle 12. tropical climate

Tourism in Antarctica

During the two-year period between 1977 and 1979, some 11,000 tourists were flown over Antarctica on Air New Zealand and Qantas Boeing 747s and DC 10s. After their 11-hour flight, tourists spent about 90 minutes flying over the continent. These excursions ended, however, when a DC 10 crashed into Mount Erebus, killing all the passengers and crew. Other countries sent tourists to Antarctica via cruise ships. People from the United States, West Germany, Spain, Argentina, and Chile accounted for 17,000 visitors by the end of the seventies.

While tourism can be good for a country's economy and employment, it can also cause numerous problems. Listed below are some problems that could be encountered if unlimited tourism were allowed in Antarctica. On the lines provided complete the statements. Choose from the list in the box that follows. Be sure to use correct punctuation.

calls for more places to dispose of them
erode vegetation, rocks, and paths
pose a threat to wildlife
suffer from disturbance by tourists
bring diseases which can kill Antarctic life
causes air pollution
tend to spoil the place they are visiting
are built in styles that do not match the landscape

1. Too many tourists ____________________
2. Hotels, restaurants, and shops ____________________
3. An increase in cars and airplanes ____________________
4. Litter can ____________________
5. Increased sewage and waste materials ____________________
6. Tourists can unwittingly ____________________
7. Penguin rookeries ____________________
8. Trampling tourists' feet ____________________

Answers (Fold under before copying.)

1. tend to spoil the place they are visiting. 2. are built in styles that do not match the landscape. 3. causes air pollution. 4. pose a threat to wildlife. 5. calls for more places to dispose of them. 6. bring diseases which can kill Antarctic life. 7. suffer from disturbance by tourists. 8. erode vegetation, rocks, and paths.

Vietnam Reunified

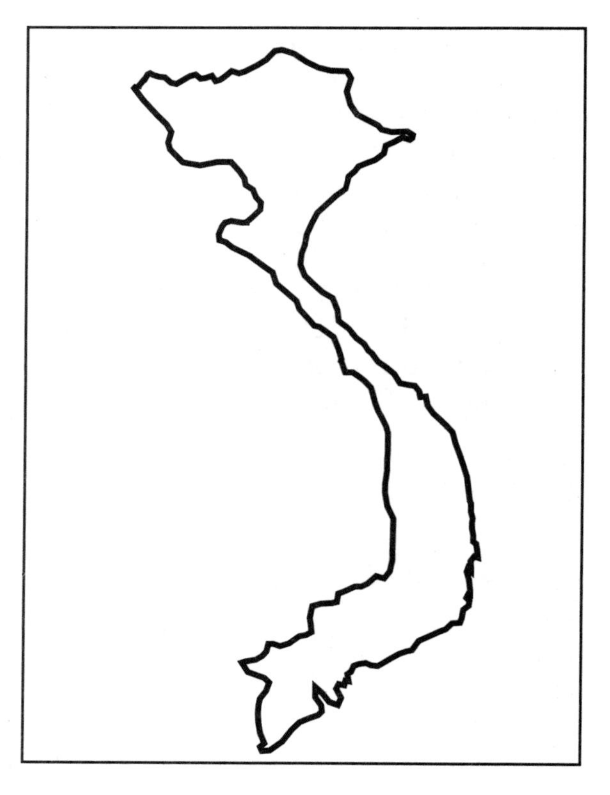

In 1973 the United States and North Vietnam reached a cease-fire agreement, and the last American combat personnel were withdrawn. But the peace was short-lived, elections were not held, and by 1974 the war between North and South Vietnam resumed. On April 18, 1975, Secretary of State Henry Kissinger, sensing the end of the war, ordered the evacuation of all remaining Americans from South Vietnam. *Operation Frequent Wind* evacuated close to 7,000 people, including 1400 Americans. On April 30, 1975, North Vietnamese troops arrived in Saigon, and South Vietnam quickly surrendered. As North Vietnamese tanks made their way to the United States' headquarters there, a few hundred remaining Marines and civilians gathered on the building's rooftop. Helicopters plucked them up and airlifted them to waiting warships. It was a chaotic scene as thousands of South Vietnamese men, women, and children, many of whom had been allies of the United States, filled the street around the headquarters. They fought and pleaded with officials to be taken away by helicopter, but there was not enough room for them.

When General Duong Van Minh announced the surrender of South Vietnam and the reunification of Vietnam, it had been 20 years since the Geneva Accords which called for an end to foreign rule and free elections for reunification. Many Americans wondered what had been accomplished by the long years of U.S. support and involvement.

Suggested Activities

Chronology Make a chronology of important events in the war in Vietnam during the 1970s.

Evaluate Write a list of lessons the United States might have learned from its involvement in the Vietnam conflict.

Unofficial War Explain how the United States could carry on such a large war operation in Vietnam despite the fact that no war was officially declared by Congress.

Chart Construct a chart of the Viet Cong and the Army of the Republic of Vietnam. Compare their leaders, losses, and countries which backed them.

Current Relations Explore current U.S. relations with Vietnam to learn whether time has healed the wounds between the two countries.

Memorial On November 11, 1982, the Vietnam Veterans Memorial was unveiled in Washington, D.C., to commemorate the 58,000 American lives lost in Vietnam between 1959 and 1975. Find a picture of the memorial and draw your own design for a suitable memorial.

Islamic Revolution

By 1978, opposition to the Shah of Iran, Mohammed Reza Pahlavi, had reached monumental proportions. He was attacked for his excessive personal lifestyle and was condemned for the corruption in his government. Rapid industrial growth had been offset by a decline in agriculture; 35 percent of the country's food had to be imported. In addition, the Islamic clergy was unhappy with the reforms and restraints on their powers.

Western influences were considered an insult to Islam. Many Iranians blamed the increasing inflation rate on the United States support of the Shah. Amid mass demonstrations and civil unrest, the Shah was forced to flee the country in 1978.

Ayatollah Khomeini returned from exile to lead the Islamic Revolution and easily took over power in Iran in February 1979. One of his first acts was to proclaim the country an Islamic Republic. He vowed to rid the nation of all Western influences and instituted a strict code of Islamic behavior. Severe punishment awaited anyone who broke these laws. A difficult period followed as unemployment rose and ethnic unrest erupted with the Kurds in northwestern Iran. A severe drop in the production of oil caused a panic among the industrialized countries. Anti-Western feeling continued to increase in the following months.

While the Western world was dealing with the women's movement and increasing its recognition of women's roles in society, the Islamic movement did just the opposite. Under Khomeini's rule, women had to wear traditional garb and keep their hair, and at certain times their faces, covered. Women were not allowed to own the clothes they wore, nor did they have rights over their children. There was little or no protection against a violent husband. In fact, a husband who killed his wife could go free unless the wife's family could pay a large price for his death sentence. A man could marry many wives, and he could order his wife out of the house or divorce her without even telling her.

On the lines below, explore one of these topics:

1 Explain why you think such fundamentalism would or would not work in Western countries.
2. Tell how you think the women's movement would be greeted by men and women in Islamic countries.

____

____

____

____

____

____

The Sydney Opera House

Construction of the Sydney Opera House began in 1958, and by 1973 it was completed. Read about this magnificent structure, one of the architectural wonders of the world. Then complete the exercise that follows.

One of the most famous and unusual buildings in Australia is the Sydney Opera House. Designed by Danish architect Jorn Utzon, it is set in the largest natural harbor in the world. This impressive concrete and glass structure has a roof designed to look like sails on a ship and a body that resembles a ship's body. Inside there is a full-size concert hall, an opera theatre, a smaller theatre, an auditorium, and a film-screening theatre. Classical operas, plays, ballets, and concerts are performed there. Several companies are headquartered there, including the Australian Ballet, the Sydney Symphony Orchestra, and the Australian Opera Company.

Problems with the building's sails caused construction costs to soar from an estimated seven million dollars to 102 million. It was a difficult task and required workers to climb up the slippery roof by using ropes. Afterwards, the laborers worked by sitting in small chairs with safety belts around their waists.

Small individual tiles were cemented to large tile lids which in turn were bolted to the shell structure. In all, more than one million small tiles covering 4,000 lids were attached to the building with 10,000 bronze bolts. Glass covers the inside of the sails, and there are more than 2,000 double-thick glass windowpanes.

In September of 1973, the Sydney Opera House was completed and in a grand ceremony was opened by Queen Elizabeth of England.

Read each statement below. Circle **I** if the information can be inferred from the paragraphs. Circle **O** if the statement expresses an opinion. Be prepared to defend your answers.

1. I O The Sydney Opera House is a beautiful structure.
2. I O It took many years to build the Sydney Opera House.
3. I O Work on the roof was tedious and difficult.
4. I O Utzon's design for the building was a good one.
5. I O The building is soundproof.
6. I O Construction costs were high.
7. I O A variety of events can be conducted at the Opera House.
8. I O Movies can be seen at the Opera House.

Answers (Fold under before copying.) These are suggested answers. Accept any answers which the students can successfully defend.

1. O 2. I 3. I 4. O 5. O 6. I 7. I 8. I

An English Painter and Photographer

David Hockney is the best known British artist of his time. A realistic painter, Hockney often incorporates photography within the composition of his paintings. Bold colors are typical of his work which is often inspired by the blue skies of Southern California.

Born in 1937 in Bradford, England, to a working class family, David Hockney attended local schools. When he was 16 years old, he enrolled at the Bradford School of Art and studied there for four years. His early training focused on traditional art, but that changed when he entered London's Royal College of Art. Hockney was influenced by an American pop artist and soon he began to develop his own distinguishable style. In 1961 he won a major art award from his college and first prize at an exhibition in Liverpool. Two years later he won international recognition with a series of etchings, *A Rake's Progress*. By 1970 Hockney's art was in demand, particularly in the United States. In England his 1977 autobiography became a bestseller.

Some critics classify Hockney's work as op art, but he gradually changed his artistic focus as his career progressed. His style evolved from that of painting to that of a creator of photographic collages. In this type of collage different photographic images are used to create one picture, and several optical images are combined to create one point of view.

No matter what his style or medium, David Hockney continues to be a popular artist.

Suggested Activities

Art Project

Explore some of Hockney's work. Many fine art books may be available at your local library or bookstore. Also check gift stores that sell art calendars which feature specific artists. Discuss the images and colors present in his work. Follow up with the art project below.

Materials: old magazines, scissors, white drawing paper, glue, colored pencils or markers

Directions: Look through the magazines to find a picture that interests them.
Cut out the picture and glue it to the drawing paper.
Complete the rest of the scene with colored pencils or markers.

Irish Peace Activists

In 1977 the Nobel Peace Prize was awarded to two women, Mairead Corrigan and Betty Williams, for their role in reconciling Northern Ireland's two warring sides. Drawn together by a tragic accident, the two women joined forces to begin a peace movement. Below is a look at their lives and how two ordinary citizens won worldwide acclaim.

Mairead Corrigan **Betty Willams**

Mairead Corrigan

Mairead Corrigan was born in 1944 to working-class parents in a Catholic section of West Belfast, Northern Ireland. The second child in a family of five girls and two boys, she attended Catholic school until she was 14 years old. Then she joined the Legion of Mary, a Catholic organization devoted to helping others, and continued as a volunteer with the society into her adult years. Corrigan strongly opposed the strife that was occurring between the Catholics and the Protestants in Northern Ireland. Roman Catholics there wanted to be free of British rule while the Protestants sided with Great Britain. In 1976, Corrigan came face to face with the violence when her sister and her sister's three children were hit by a runaway IRA car. All three children were killed, and Corrigan, along with her brother-in-law, appeared on television to condemn the IRA's actions.

Betty Williams

Born in a Catholic section of Belfast in 1942, Betty Williams had a mother who was Catholic and a father who was Protestant. Tolerance was advocated in their household; there was no room for bigotry. At 13, she took on the responsibility of raising her younger sister after their mother suffered a debilitating stroke. Later, Williams became a secretary. On August 10, 1976, she witnessed the accident that killed Mairead Corrigan's three nieces. Determined to do something to facilitate a peaceful solution to the two sides' differences, Betty Williams drafted a petition and went from door to door collecting 6,000 signatures. After presenting the petition on television, she and Mairead Corrigan joined forces.

That fall, the two women led tens of thousands of Belfast women on peace marches. Corrigan and Williams were harassed, beaten, and threatened, but still they did not give up. They even traveled to foreign countries, including Australia, Canada, and the United States, to spread the word about their peace movement. Violence in Northern Ireland decreased by 54 percent during this period, and in 1977 Corrigan and Williams became the first women to win the Nobel Peace Prize since 1944.

Suggested Activity

Discussion Discuss the following questions:

What is the current status between Catholics and Protestants in Northern Ireland?

What is the IRA and when was it founded?

Why have Protestants and Catholics been fighting in Northern Ireland for the past 70 years?

The Loch Ness Monster

Loch Ness is a famous lake located in the northern part of Scotland. According to an ancient legend, a monster lives in the lake, but there were no reported sightings until 1933. The first photograph of the creature was taken after a new road was constructed on the lake's north shore. The shadowy figure was named the Loch Ness Monster, or Nessie for short. In the 1960s sonar equipment was used to search the lake's bottom, but nothing unusual turned up. An underwater camera in 1972 did photograph some type of creature, but experts still aren't sure what it is. Scientists think it could be a sea cow, floating logs, or possibly a pesiosaur from the dinosaur era. Whatever it is, the lake attracts thousands of visitors yearly, all of whom are waiting for a glimpse of the elusive Loch Ness Monster.

Learn some facts about the lake itself. Use the code in the box below to help you supply the missing letters in the words.

b=7	f=16	j=10	m=13	r=14	v=6
c=12	g=3	k=9	n=17	s=2	w=1
d=4	h=15	l=8	p=5	t=18	z=11

1. ___(8) o ___(12) ___(15)   ___(17) e ___(2) ___(2)   i ___(2)   22   ___(13) i ___(8) e ___(2)   o ___(14)   35   ___(9) ___(13)

___(8) o ___(17) ___(3)   a ___(17) ___(4)   a ___(7) ou ___(18)   1   ___(13) i ___(8) e   o ___(14)   1.6   ___(9) ___(13)   ___(1) i ___(4) e.

2. ___(5) a ___(14) ___(18) ___(2)   o ___(16)   ___(18) ___(15) e   ___(8) a ___(9) e   a ___(14) e   ___(13) o ___(14) e   ___(18) ___(15) a ___(17)

700   ___(16) ee ___(18)   o ___(14)   213   ___(13)   ___(4) ee ___(5).

3. ___(18) ___(15) e   ___(8) a ___(9) e   ___(17) e ___(6) e ___(14)   ___(16) ___(14) ee ___(11) e ___(2)   ___(7) e ___(12) au ___(2) e   i ___(18)

i ___(2)   ___(2) o   ___(4) ee ___(5).

4. I ___(18) ___(2)   ___(1) a ___(18) e ___(14)   i ___(2)   ___(13) u ___(14) ___(9) y   a ___(17) ___(4)   ___(6) i ___(2) i ___(7) i ___(8) i ___(18) y

i ___(2)   ___(8) e ___(2) ___(2)   ___(18) ___(15) a ___(17)   a   ___(16) e ___(1)   ___(16) ee ___(18).

Answers (Fold under before copying.)

1. Loch Ness is 22 miles or 35 km long and about 1 mile or 1.6 km wide.
2. Parts of the lake are more than 700 feet or 213 m deep.
3. The lake never freezes because it is so deep.
4. Its water is murky and visibility is less than a few feet.

In the News

In the box below are the names of a number of newsworthy individuals from the 1970s. Choose from this list when completing any of the creative writing projects that follow.

Anwar Sadat	Leonid Brezhnev	Margaret Thatcher
David Bowie	Queen Elizabeth	Harold Wilson
Evonne Goolagong	Pierre Trudeau	Haile Selassie
Menachem Begin	Olga Korbut	Coco Chanel
Elton John	Shane Gould	Alexander Solzhenitsyn
Golda Meir	Pope John Paul II	Germaine Greer
David Hockney	Nadia Comaneci	Pablo Picasso
Mairead Corrigan	Mother Teresa	Pablo Casals
Betty Williams	Idi Amin	Colleen McCullough

1. If you had been alive during the 1970s, who is the one person you would have liked to have met? Pretend you are a reporter whose job is to interview this person. Write the questions and answers to this interview.
2. Choose any two names from the list above. Write a creative story about a time when the two might have met. Include a conversation the two might have had.
3. You are an artist or a fashion designer and very much admire the style of ___________________. Critique his or her work and write a review for a national art or fashion magazine.
4. Pick a figure who contributed something to world peace. Write a story about how and why this individual might have decided to work for the cause of world peace.
5. Choose a name from the above list and then think about this question: What are 10 important things you think others should know about this person? Write a page explaining your ideas.
6. Everyone in the list above faced problems in his or her career. After choosing a figure, think about the problems in his or her life. Identify one problem and explain how he or she solved it. Make a list of some alternative solutions to the problem that he or she might or might not have considered.
7. Write a letter to an individual you admire. Explain to him or her how you think he or she made the world a better place.
8. Choose six figures from the list above and make a set of trading cards. Each card should contain a picture and a brief description of that person's accomplishments.
9. Who is one person from the list above that you greatly admire? Think about the best thing that he or she ever did that you know about. Write a story about how this affected others in the world.
10. Write a poem about one of the people listed above. Use the poetry form of your choice—cinquain, haiku, etc.

Seventies Facts and Figures

The United States in 1970

Population:	203,235,298
National Debt:	$450 billion
Federal Minimum Wage:	rose from $2.10 per hour to $2.30 per hour in 1976 rose from $2.65 per hour to $2.90 per hour in 1979
U.S. Postage:	rose from 10 cents to 13 cents in 1975
Movies:	*French Connection, The Godfather* and *The Godfather Part II, The Sting, One Flew Over the Cuckoo's Nest, Rocky, Network, Annie Hall, The Deer Hunter, Butch Cassidy and the Sundance Kid, True Grit, Catch 22, Taxi Driver, All the President's Men, Star Wars, Saturday Night Fever, Grease, Animal House, MASH, Blazing Saddles, Jaws, American Graffiti, Sleeper, Shaft, Patton, The Bad News Bears, Love Story*
Movie Stars:	Barbra Streisand, Jane Fonda, Robert Redford, Elliot Gould, George C. Scott, Glenda Jackson, Liza Minelli, Gene Hackman, Marlon Brando, Woody Allen, Jack Lemmon, Faye Dunaway, Al Pacino, Sylvester Stallone, Louise Fletcher, Jack Nicholson, James Caan, Lily Tomlin, Alan Arkin, George Burns, Talia Shire, Jason Robards, Robert de Niro, Richard Roundtree, John Travolta, Olivia Newton John, Liv Ullman, Jodi Foster, Carrie Fisher, Vanessa Redgrave, Marsha Mason, Richard Dreyfuss, John Belushi, Cicely Tyson, Meryl Streep, Jon Voight, Dustin Hoffman
Songs:	"Bridge Over Troubled Water," "Let It Be," "Signed Sealed Delivered," "American Woman," "Joy to the World," "My Sweet Lord," "Me and Bobbie McGee," "The First Time Ever I Saw Your Face," "Lean on Me," "Crocodile Rock," "Superstition," "The Way We Were," "Annie's Song," "Sundown," "Fame," "One of These Nights," "Fifty Ways to Leave Your Lover," "You Light Up My Life," "Margaritaville," "Hotel California," "You Don't Bring Me Flowers," "Staying Alive," "I Will Survive," "We Are Family," "Raindrops Keep Falling on My Head"
Books:	*Winds of War* by Herman Wouk, *Breakfast of Champions* by Kurt Vonnegut, *Roots* by Alex Haley, *Chesapeake* by James Michener, *The Thorn Birds* by Colleen McCullough, *The Bell Jar* by Sylvia Plath, *Trinity* by Leon Uris, *Watership Down* by Richard Adams, *Jaws* by Peter Benchley, *Sophie's Choice* by William Styron
TV Programs:	*All in the Family, The Mary Tyler Moore Show, Happy Days, Saturday Night Live, The Partridge Family, The Jeffersons, The Dukes of Hazard, MASH, The Muppet Show, The Brady Bunch, Charlie's Angels, Columbo*
Fashions:	granny dresses, corduroy jeans, leather chokers and bracelets, flared pants or bellbottoms, army fatigues, Annie Hall look, designer label jeans, preppy and Ivy League styles, kaftans, Indian shirts and gauze smocks, puka shell necklaces
Fads:	home video games played on the television screen, streaking, disco music and dancing, mood rings, pet rocks, jogging, transcendental meditation, yoga

Comparing the Times

With your partner fill in the blanks on this page. Compare your answers with the information on page 81.

United States Now ________________
year

Population ____

____

National Debt ____

____

Federal Minimum Wage ____

____

United States Postage ____

____

Popular Books ____

____

Popular Movies ____

____

Popular Stars ____

____

Popular Songs ____

____

Popular TV Shows ____

____

Fashions ____

____

Fads ____

____

In Order

See how well you know the events, inventions, and people of the seventies. In each pair below choose the one that came first. Circle the letter of your choice. Research your answers using reference materials such as magazines, encylopedias, and the internet.

1. **Popular music:** a. the disco music of the Bee Gees b. glam rock of David Bowie
2. **Tennis star:** a. Billie Jean King b. Chris Evert
3. **Women's movement:** a. women's suffrage b. NOW
4. **Political scandal:** a. the Watergate affair b. the Pentagon Papers
5. **Space exploration:** a. the launch of *Skylab* b. the launch of two *Viking* space probes
6. **Newbery winner:** a. *Sounder* b. *The Slave Dancer*
7. **Middle Eastern event:** a. the formation of OPEC b. the oil crisis
8. **Event in Iran:** a. Iranian hostage crisis b. the overthrow of the Shah of Iran
9. **Ecology:** a. the first Earth Day b. the 55-miles-per-hour speed limit
10. **Event in Vietnam:** a. Vietnam is reunified b. last American soldiers leave Vietnam
11. **Movie:** a. *Jaws* b. *Star Wars*
12. **Vice president:** a. Spiro Agnew b. Walter Mondale
13. **Completion of building:** a. Sydney Opera House b. World Trade Center
14. **Popular fad:** a. mood rings and pet rocks b. disco music and dancing
15. **TV debut of:** a. *Saturday Night Live* b. miniseries *Roots*
16. **Headline news:** a. America's bicentennial b. incident at Kent State
17. **Fashion:** a. designer jeans b. the Annie Hall look
18. **Invention:** a. home video game b. food processor
19. **Technology:** a. test tube baby b. digital watches
20. **Airplane design:** a. the Concorde b. the Boeing 747
21. **Disaster:** a. explosion on *Apollo 13* b. Three Mile Island accident
22. **Event in the Middle East:** a. Yom Kippur War b. return to Islamic fundamentalism
23. **Sports:** a. the craze of jogging b. Mark Spitz wins seven gold medals
24. **Event in Central America:** a. mass suicide at Jonestown b. the United States Panama Canal Treaty
25. **Invention:** a. personal stereos b. personal computers

Newsworthy Crossword Puzzle

Each of the figures in this crossword puzzle was in the news during the seventies decade. Some were famous for their crimes while others were famous for their looks. Some gained fame through the entertainment industry, others through their politics.

Use the clues below to help you determine the correct last names. Write them in the spaces provided. Then fill in the crossword puzzle with the last name only of each figure.

Across

2. Patty _______ SLA, heiress
4. Bob _______ journalist, Watergate
5. Gloria _______ feminist, *Ms.* magazine
7. William _______ army lieutenant, My Lai Massacre
10. Muhammed _______ boxing, heavyweight champ
11. Mark _______ Seven Olympic gold medals, swimmer
13. Gary _______ murderer, execution
15. Judy _______ children's author, controversial
16. Jim _______ cult, mass suicide
18. Kareem _______ basketball, L.A. Lakers
19. Jim _______ jogging, wrote a bestseller

Down

1. Farrah _______ *Charlie's Angels*, hairstyle
3. Spiro _______ vice president, resigned from office
5. Steven _______ director, *Jaws*
6. John _______ Watergate, former attorney general
8. Evel _______ daredevil, motorcycle stunts
9. Barbara _______ first female anchor, NBC news
12. Billie Jean _______ tennis, Battle of the Sexes
14. Jimi _______ rock guitarist, drug-related death
17. Hank _______ 715 homers, Atlanta Braves

What Year Was That?

Check how well you remember the events of the seventies with this quiz. After each number read the three clues given. Decide in which year all three events occurred and circle the year of your answer.

1. Elvis Presley dies. The United States admits nearly 200,000 Southeast Asian refugees. The first personal computers are introduced.

   a. 1975 b. 1976 c. 1977

2. The first Earth Day is celebrated. Four student protestors are killed at Kent State. The first female generals are appointed.

   a. 1970 b. 1971 c. 1972

3. Arabs begin an oil embargo. Vice President Spiro Agnew resigns. The military draft ends.

   a. 1971 b. 1972 c. 1973

4. *Mariner 9* orbits Mars. The first microprocessor is patented. The science of sociobiology is founded.

   a. 1971 b. 1972 c. 1973

5. Former Vice President Humphrey dies. A ruling is made in the Bakke case. Sony introduces the walkman, a personal stereo cassette player.

   a. 1977 b. 1978 c. 1979

6. President Carter and Soviet leader Breshnev sign Salt II. *Skylab* crashes in Australia. The Three Mile Island nuclear plant malfunctions.

   a. 1977 b. 1978 c. 1979

7. President Ford raises tariffs on oil imports. Mauna Loa erupts in Hawaii. Two assassination attempts are made on President Ford.

   a. 1974 b. 1975 c. 1976

8. The Pentagon Papers reveal a government cover up about Vietnam. The Twenty-sixth Amendment becomes law. *Apollo 14* goes to the moon.

   a. 1971 b. 1972 c. 1973

9. UPC bar codes first appear on food products. President Nixon resigns. *People* magazine debuts.

   a. 1972 b. 1973 c. 1974

10. The United States celebrates its bicentennial. *Viking I* lands on Mars. Jimmy Carter is elected president.

    a. 1974 b. 1975 c. 1976

11. The United States Department of Energy is established. The Trans-Alaska Pipeline is in use. The United States and Panama sign a canal treaty.

    a. 1977 b. 1978 c. 1979

12. The last United States combat troops leave Vietnam. Alabama governor George Wallace is shot in an assassination attempt. DDT is banned.

    a. 1971 b. 1972 c. 1973

Into the Eighties

- President Jimmy Carter leaves the presidency. On his last day in office, American hostages in Iran are finally released after more than a year in captivity. The release dovetails with the inauguration of President Ronald Reagan.
- Pope John Paul II is shot, but he recovers and gains the admiration of the world by forgiving his attacker. President Ronald Reagan is also shot, and he, too, recovers. A third victim, Indira Gandhi, Prime Minister of India, is shot and killed by her bodyguards.
- Rock musician John Lennon is shot and killed in front of his New York apartment. Millions of fans grieve his loss.
- Britain and Argentina go to war over the Falkland Islands. The United States invades Panama and Grenada and bombs Libyan terrorist bases. Israel forces the PLO from Lebanon. Iran and Iraq go to war. Russia continues its occupation of Afghanistan for nearly a decade.
- A new strategic defense initiative called "Star Wars" gains momentum. The world superpowers agree to reduce nuclear missiles.
- Famine in Ethiopia kills millions. Many make great efforts to relieve the famine, most notably rock musician Bob Geldof and his concert called Live Aid, which earns millions for relief.
- Mikhail Gorbachev comes to power in Russia, bringing about a push toward democracy.
- A nuclear power reactor explodes in Chernobyl, Russia, killing and wounding thousands. The effects of the blast are far-reaching.
- Chinese students in Tiananmen Square protest the government in China. Many are killed by government soldiers who squelch the uprising.
- The Soviet Union begins to unravel, and numerous Soviet bloc countries overthrow communism. The Berlin Wall comes down, and East and West Germany are unified.
- The world's stock markets crash. Insider trading scandals rock the financial world.
- Congress holds hearings over the Iran-Contra affair, uncovering a secret arms deal with American antagonist Iran. Marine Lieutenant Colonel Oliver North admits secretly funneling money to the Contras, an army of Nicaraguan rebels.
- Sandra Day O'Connor becomes the first female American Supreme Court Justice. Sally Ride becomes the first American woman in space. Elizabeth Dole becomes the first woman to head the U.S. Department of Transportation. Geraldine Ferraro becomes the first female candidate on a major party ticket for the office of vice president.
- Technology revolutionizes the American home with personal computers, VCR's, compact disc players, and more.
- Terrorism around the world is on the rise with a number of skyjackings, bombings, and hostage situations, most for political reasons.
- The battle against apartheid continues in South Africa and around the world.
- Corazón Aquino is elected Philippine president, replacing President Ferdinand Marcos who is implicated in the murder of Aquino's husband, a former presidential hopeful.
- Human Immunodeficiency Virus (HIV), a retrovirus, is discovered to be the cause of Acquired Immune Deficiency Syndrome (AIDS). The first permanent artificial heart is placed in a patient.

Literature Connections

One surefire way to interest students in a specific topic is through the use of children's literature. Read through the annotated bibliographies on this and the next two pages to help you decide which pieces of literature you might like to use with your class. Helpful suggestions for extending the pages follow each description.

Drylongso by Virginia Hamilton (Harcourt Brace Jovanovich 1992)

Summary The setting of this tale is the small town of Osfield in the western part of Mississippi during 1975. It is a period of drought much like the one that hit the Midwest during the Great Depression. One day a young boy, Drylongso, emerges out of the wall of dust surrounding the town. He stays for a while and helps one family by finding water. All too soon he decides it is time to move on. Lindy, the heroine of the story, is sad to see him go, but he has accomplished his goal of leaving the family better off than when he first arrived.

Extensions

Causes Ask the students to name some causes of drought. Discuss the causes of the dust that enveloped the town of Osfield.

Extend As an extension of the previous activity, have the students write cause and effect statements about drought and the ensuing dust, e.g., Because it had not rained in so long, the grass dried up. Have students identify the cause and the effect in each of their statements.

Comparisons With the class compare the drought situation of Osfield with the Dust Bowl of the Great Depression. Which of the two events affected a larger portion of the country? Which of the two events lasted longer and did more property damage? Construct a class chart showing how the two events were alike and different. As an alternative, compare a dust storm with a snow storm and explain ways in which the two are similar, e.g., both have drifts; both can blind a person.

Tall Tale Read aloud Drylongso's story about the pilot who got caught in a dust storm. Direct the students to write their own tall tale about getting caught in a dust storm, or ask them to complete the following story starter: It was so dry that . . . .

Response Copy this quote from page 49 onto the board and have the students respond in writing: "'But remember', said Mamalou, 'when he was born his mama said that where he goes life will grow better.'"

How To How-to books were popular in the seventies. Divide the students into groups and have them write a how-to brochure about dowsing for water.

Creative Writing Pair or group the students and direct them to write a sequel to this story to be titled *Wetlongso.*

Literature Connections *(cont.)*

Assign the class to read some literature selections popular during the 1970s.

Julie of the Wolves by Jean Craighead George (Harper Row, 1972)

Summary Miyax, an Eskimo girl, lives in Alaska with her father from whom she learns her people's traditions and customs. Soon enough it is time for her to attend school. Leaving camp for the first time, Miyax lives with her aunt in civilization, but she begins to feel ashamed of her people's old-fashioned ways. A correspondence with a pen pal, Amy, helps Miyax escape from her increasingly unbearable life.

When Miyax is just 13, her life becomes even worse when she is forced into an arranged marriage. After her husband, Daniel, assaults her, Miyax sets out for San Francisco. All does not go well as she finds herself lost in the vast tundra and out of food. How she manages to survive is a story of courage and self-discovery that will keep students engrossed until the conclusion of this exciting novel.

Extensions

Wolves After completing the book, discuss with the students what they learned about wolf behavior from this novel. On chart paper make a web of their responses. What other questions do they have about wolves? Use a pen of a different color to record these questions around the web. Assign different pairs or groups to research answers and have students write them on the corresponding section of the web.

Geography Each pair of students will need a globe or an atlas, a ruler, and a length of string for this activity. Direct them to measure the distance from Julie's location to San Francisco by land. Tell students to plan a route for her to travel by sea and measure that distance, too. As a class, discuss which is the best route for Julie to take. Ask students to defend their choices.

Vocabulary Development As students read the book, tell them to keep a list of difficult words. Some ways to use the words:

1. Students can create their own crossword puzzles or word search puzzles to be exchanged with partners.
2. Groups can make an illustrated dictionary of the words.
3. The class can play charades, acting out the vocabulary words.

Lost Being lost is a truly frightening experience. Think about how Julie handled herself when she found herself lost in the tundra with no one to help her and no modern conveniences to enable her to find a safe return. Ask students how they think they would have handled such a situation. Talk about a time when they were lost, how they felt, and how they were able to return to safety.

Predictions Ask the class to predict some of the events that will happen to Miyax after she returns to her father. Instruct the students to use some of the events to write an epilogue for *Julie of the Wolves.*

Literature Connections *(cont.)*

The Slave Dancer by Paula Fox (Dell, 1975)

Summary The setting is New Orleans in 1840. Young Jessie Bollier spends his time wandering about the fruit stalls by the river, playing his fife for pennies. One day, he is kidnapped by sailors and brought on board *The Moonlight* to be a slave dancer. Life on *The Moonlight,* a slaving ship bound for Africa, is distressing as Jessie sees cruelty he has never before experienced. He must play the fife while the slaves are forced to exercise to his music.

Extensions

Slavery Write the word "slavery" on the board. Discuss its meaning with the class. Ask students if the practice is ever justified. How do they think it would feel to be a slave? How would they feel if they were forced to watch others being treated as slaves?

Relationships On the board or overhead projector, draw a circle and write the name "Jessie" inside it. Draw six spokes around the circle and write a different character's name on each one: Aunt Agatha, Clay Purvis, Benjamin Stout, Captain Cawthorne, Ras, and Daniel. Discuss Jessie's relationship with each of these characters and add the information to the graphic.

Research *The Slave Dancer* is fiction, but it is based on historical fact. With the class make a chart of "Fact" and "Fiction." List story events, people, and places under each category. Assign the students to research this information and compare it to the class fact and fiction chart. Change the information as necessary.

Point of View Ask the students to explain why Purvis and Claudius kidnapped Jessie from his hometown. From their point of view, they were justified in their actions. Have students explain why. Let the students explain and justify other story events from the other person's point of view. Some events to discuss: Stout drops Jessie's fife into the cargo hold filled with slaves, black chiefs sell other blacks into slavery, Captain Cawthorne orders the remaining slaves to be thrown overboard in shark territory, the captain packs nearly 100 Africans into a tiny cargo space.

Geography Each pair of students will need a map or globe. Direct students to use their knowledge from the story to trace the route Jessie takes from his home to Africa.

Ship's Log Captain Cawthorne kept a log of the day's events. What if Ras had one, also? Choose a story event that occurred on board the ship. Fold a sheet of paper in half. On one half of the paper write a diary entry for Captain Cawthorne. Write Ras's version of the same event on the other half of the page.

Water Rationing On good days, half a pint of water per person was one day's rationing. Group the students and have them measure half a pint of water. How many cups is that? If water were rationed in the classroom, how much would be needed for the entire class? *Alternate Activity:* Tell the students to keep a written record of how much water they drink in one day. Compare that amount to the amount allotted the sailors on board *The Moonlight.*

Group Writing Projects

This page lists eight different creative writing projects that can be assigned to large or small groups. Give students a choice of assignments. Let the groups present their completed projects to the rest of the class.

Pet Rocks Pet rocks were a popular fad in the seventies. They came packaged in their own carryall with a set of tongue-in-cheek directions for their care and were priced at just $5 each. With your group go outside to find a suitable rock. Create a container for the rock, name your pet, and write directions for the care and feeding of the rock.

Inventions All of the following were invented during the seventies: Sony Walkman personal cassette players, pocket calculators, inexpensive (under $10) digital watches, video games played on the TV screen, prerecorded video cassettes, and miniature TV screens. Pretend it is the year 2025 and you are writing about inventions of the 1990s. Make a catalog of these innovations complete with pictures and descriptions of how each is used.

How To How-to books were popular in the seventies. As a group determine a topic that interests you and write a how-to book. Some suggested titles include *How to Write a Term Paper, How to Look Good on a Budget, How to Make Friends, How to Disco Dance.*

T-Shirts In the mid-seventies plain T-shirts were out and T-shirts decorated with words or slogans were in. Brainstorm a list of words or phrases that might have been popular in the seventies. Think of events then such as Watergate, the oil embargo, the Twenty-sixth Amendment, etc. Draw and cut out large T-shirt shapes from a piece of butcher paper and decorate each one with some seventies lingo and/or pictures.

The Environment With your partners brainstorm a list of things you can do to clean up and protect the environment at home or at school on a daily basis. Create a group book using 25 of these ideas. Draw pictures to illustrate the ideas.

CB Lingo Citizen band radios were popular during the seventies, especially among truckers. They invented their own vocabulary or lingo to communicate with one another. Divide the students into groups, and direct them to make a dictionary of CB terms and their meanings. You may be able to find a prepared list of terms from a CB supply store. Check your phone book for possible sources.

Fads Mood rings were another popular fad of the seventies. Group the students and instruct them to invent a new fad for the seventies. Tell the groups to draw a picture of this new fad and develop an advertising poster that will prompt others to purchase the item.

Special Effects The 1977 movie *Star Wars* set a new standard for visual effects in motion pictures. With the students brainstorm some of the new visual effects that are currently being used in films. Have pairs of students write about an innovative special effect for the next decade. For example, smellovision would allow movie goers to smell what is on the screen, from the exhaust of cars to the food the characters eat.

Report Topics

Although a great many topics have been addressed in this book about the 1970s, there are plenty more to be discussed. Below are some additional topics for you to explore. Choose one and write about it.

- the dramatic return to strict religious fundamentalism among people of the Muslim countries such as Iran, Iraq, Libya, and Pakistan
- Jerry Falwell, the Moral Majority, and their role in politics
- the accident at the Three Mile Island nuclear power plant and the antinuclear movement that ensued
- the causes, symptoms, and treatment of Legionnaire's disease
- the benefits of transcendental meditation
- why the metric system was not embraced by the United States despite Congress' direction
- Patty Hearst and her abduction by the SLA
- Berry Gordy, the formation of Motown, and its prominent artists
- baseball great Hank Aaron who broke Babe Ruth's home run record
- the continuing impact of the *Roe v. Wade* decision
- drug-related deaths of singers Jimi Hendrix, Jim Morrison of the Doors, Elvis Presley, and Janis Joplin
- the Khmer Rouge regime in Cambodia
- *Roots* and its portrayal of African Americans
- special effects and new technology in the movie *Star Wars*
- affirmative action, the pros and cons of the policy, and who benefits most
- the aftermath of the race riots in Soweto in South Africa
- why the boat people fled Vietnam and the countries to which they emigrated
- the controversy over the followers of Sun Myung Moon, called Moonies, and their tactics
- how the Trans-Alaska Pipeline eased the oil crisis
- Proposition 13, a California measure, and why it was instituted
- the impact of the punk rock movement on the music world
- Polish union leader Lech Walesa and his fight for Solidarity
- the movie *Animal House* and the craze that it sparked
- the reign of Idi Amin and why he was made fun of by the Western world
- how the mini-series *Roots* sparked and boosted African Americans' pride in their culture
- the health benefits offered by jogging
- the United States involvement with the Sandanistas in Nicaragua
- the debate about capital punishment in the wake of Gary Gilmore's execution
- why President Carter signed a treaty to return the Panama Canal to Panama by the year 2000
- Nobel Prize winner Alexander Solzhenitsyn and his account of the Soviet prisons system
- the women's movement and how it changed women's role in society
- American sentiment toward returning Vietnam soldiers

CB Lingo

Beginning in 1977 CB (citizen band) radios were popular with truck drivers and hobbyists throughout the United States. Although they were a great communication tool, they did cause a problem when voices from highway airwaves interfered with regular radio and television frequencies. Congress and the CB manufacturers had to work together to solve the dilemma. In the meantime, CB users developed their own lingo or language to employ when they talked on their radios.

The left column below contains some common phrases used by truckers and hobbyists. At the right are the translations of these phrases. See how much CB lingo you understand by writing the letters of the phrases in Column A next to their corresponding translations in Column B. Use the lines provided.

Column A	**Column B**
a. good buddy	1. female CBer _______
b. handle	2. any policeman _______
c. breaker, breaker	3. highway clear of police _______
d. hammer	4. motorcycle _______
e. a smokey	5. congested road condition _______
f. 10-4	6. unmarked police car _______
g. Got a copy?	7. friendly term used between CBers _______
h. negatory	8. Did you hear me? _______
i. all clean	9. CBer who talks too much _______
j. bear	10. your code name _______
k. breaking up	11. no _______
l. fuzz buster	12. ok, message received _______
m. pedal to the metal	13. radar detecting device _______
n. parking lot	14. accelerator _______
o. green and clean	15. full speed _______
p. sweet thing	16. a state police _______
q.plain wrapper	17. signal loud and clear _______
r. bodacious	18. no police in sight _______
s. ratchet jaw	19. signal not clear _______
t. two wheeler	20. permission to use the channel _______

New to the Seventies

New inventions, habits, lifestyles, and occupations cause people to invent new words, but sometimes events can spawn new vocabulary, too. Listed below are some of the words and phrases that came into popular use during the seventies.

Affirmative Action This term refers to the policy of giving extra consideration to minorities when hiring new employees.

CB This is an abbreviation for citizen band radio which truckers use to communicate with one another. They developed their own shorthand terms which they use when talking.

Cult This term refers to a religion or religious sect whose members often blindly follow the dictates of one powerful leader.

Détente A political term, détente means a relaxation of strained relations. During the 1970s the U.S.S.R. and the U.S. reached détente in their political relationship.

Embargo This term means to impose a restriction on trade. In 1973 the Arabs issued an oil embargo against the Western world.

ERA This abbreviation stands for the Equal Rights Amendment. Designed to give equal rights to women, it never gained the necessary state support to be ratified.

Feminism This is the women's movement which worked to win full and equal rights and respect for women in society.

"Get my head together" This expression meant that a person was trying to sort out his or her feelings and attempting to find fulfillment with his or her life.

Glam Rock Rock artists put glamour into rock with elaborate costumes and makeup. David Bowie's character Ziggy Stardust was the epitome of glam rock.

Graffiti This is the name given to pictures and words spray-painted or scribbled on walls, advertising posters, freeways, etc.

Gridlock This term means a traffic jam in which no vehicular traffic is possible.

Microprocessors These are integrated circuits on a single chip which contain the central processing unit of a computer.

Oil Crisis This worldwide economic crisis was brought on when Arab oil-producing nations drastically cut production and sharply raised the prices of oil. What followed was a shortage of oil, loss of production, and high inflation and unemployment rates.

SALT This acronym stands for Strategic Arms Limitation Talks. These discussions between the United States and the U.S.S.R. helped to limit nuclear arms.

Sociobiology This term means the study of animal societies.

Watergate Scandal After some of Nixon's aides were apprehended breaking into Democratic headquarters in the Watergate building, the whole scandal was named after the building.

Whistle blower This refers to an individual who brings wrong doing within an organization to light.

Software in the Classroom

More and more software is finding its way into the classroom. Many of the multimedia packages allow students to access photos, speeches, film clips, maps, and newspapers of various eras in history. Although a program may not be written specifically for the topic you are studying, existing software may be adapted for your purposes. Use these suggestions to get maximum usage from these programs and to learn how to keep up with technology.

Software

American Heritage: *The History of the United States for Young People*. Byron Preiss Multimedia

American History CD. Multi-Educator

Compton's Encyclopedia of American History. McGraw Hill

The Chronicle. Sunburst Communications

Compton's Interactive Encyclopedia from Compton's New Media, Inc. The Cruncher. Microsoft Works

Blockbuster Video Guide to Movies & Videos. Creative Multimedia

Encarta (various editions). Microsoft Home

Ideas That Changed the World. Ice Publishing

Our Times: Multimedia Encyclopedia of the 20th Century (Vicarious Point of View Series 2.0). Scholastic

Presidents: A Picture History of Our Nation. National Geographic

Time Almanac. Compact Publishing, available through Broderbund, 800-922-9204

TimeLiner from Tom Snyder Productions, 800-342-0236

Time Traveler CD! Orange Cherry

Vital Links. Educational Resources (includes videodisc and audio cassette)

Where in America's Past is Carmen Sandiego? Broderbund

Using the Programs

After the initial excitement of using a new computer program wears off, you can still motivate students by letting them use the programs in different ways.

1. Print out a copy of a time line for the seventies for each group of students. Assign each group a different topic, e.g., entertainment, politics, etc. Direct the groups to research their topics and add text and pictures to their time lines.
2. Let each pair of students choose a specific photo from the 1970s. Have them research the event and write a news story to go with the picture.
3. Not enough computers? Hook your computer up to a TV screen for large-group activities or pair the students and let them take turns typing. Keep a kitchen timer handy. For more ideas see *Managing Technology in the Classroom* from Teacher Created Materials or the booklet *101+ Ways to Use a Computer in the Classroom* (Oxbow Creek Technology Committee, Oxbow Creek School, 6050 109th Ave. N., Champlin, MN 55316).

Internet

If you have access to the Internet, let the students search for related information. First ask the students to brainstorm a list of keywords or topics. Use a Web browser like Alta Vista or Web Crawler to search for sites. Facts, pictures, and sound clips are only a click away. As an alternative, you may wish to preview sites and provide students with a list of URL's for access.

Note: If the students will be searching, you may wish to install a filtering program, like *SurfWatch* from Spyglass, to limit access to objectionable material. Check with your internet service provider.

Keeping Current

To keep current with the ever-expanding list of available software programs, you may have to turn to a number of sources, including the ones below.

Magazines: *Instructor* and *Learning* (technology review columns and feature articles)

Children's Software Revue 520 North Adams Street Ypsilanti, Michigan 48197-2482 (Write for a free sample.)

PC Family and PC Kids (available at newsstands)

Books: *Great Teaching and the One-Computer Classroom* (Tom Snyder Productions, Inc., 800-342-0236)

Internet for Kids! by Ted Pederson and Francis Moss (Price Stern Sloan, Inc., 1995)

That's Edutainment! by Eric Brown (Osborne/McGraw, 1994)

Bibliography

Fiction

Note: *All titles followed by an asterisk are Newbery Award winners of the decade.*

Armstrong, William H. *Sounder.* Harper, 1970*.

Blume, Judy. *Are You There, God? It's Me, Margaret.* Bradbury, 1970.

Byars, Betsy. *Summer of the Swans.* Viking, 1970*.

Cooper, Susan. *The Grey King.* Atheneum, 1976*.

Fox, Paula. *The Slave Dancer.* Bradbury, 1974*.

George, Jean Craighead. *Julie of the Wolves.* Harper, 1973*.

Hamilton, Virginia. *Drylongso.* Harcourt Brace Jovanovich, 1992.

——*M.C. Higgins the Great.* Macmillan, 1975*.

Kellogg, Steven. *Pinkerton, Behave.* Dial, 1979.

Korman, Gordon. *This Can't Be Happening at Macdonald Hall.* Scholastic, 1975.

O'Brien, Robert C. *Mrs. Frisby and the Rats of NIMH.* Atheneum, 1972*.

Paterson, Katherine. *Bridge to Terabithia.* Crowell, 1978*.

Raskin, Ellen. *The Westing Game.* Dutton, 1979*.

Rodgers, Mary. *Freaky Friday.* Harper, 1972.

Taylor, Mildred D. *Roll of Thunder, Hear My Cry.* Dial, 1977*.

Nonfiction

Aaseng, Nathan. *You Are the President.* Oliver Press, 1994.

Anderson, Dave. *The Story of the Olympics.* A Beech Tree Paperback Book, 1996.

Ashby, Ruth and Ohrn, Deborah Gore, ed. *Herstory: Women Who Changed the World.* Viking, 1995.

Duden, Jane. *Timelines: 1970s.* Crestwood House, 1989.

Grun, Bernard. *The Timetables of History.* A Touchstone Book, 1991.

Hakim, Joy. *All the People.* Oxford University Press, 1995.

Hopkinson, Christina. *The Twentieth Century.* Usborne Publishing Ltd., 1993.

Johnson, David E. *From Day to Day: A Calendar of Notable Birthdays and Events.* The Scarecrow Press, Inc., 1990.

Leder, Jane. *Grace & Glory, A Century of Women in the Olympics.* Triumph Books, 1996.

Mayo, Edith P., ed. *The Smithsonian Book of the First Ladies.* Henry Holt and Company, 1996.

Morrison, Marion. *The Amazon Rainforest and Its People.* Thomson Learning, 1993.

Rubel, David. *Scholastic Encyclopedia of the Presidents and Their Times.* Scholastic, Inc., 1994.

——*The United States in the 20th Century.* Scholastic, Inc., 1995.

Teacher Created Materials

#064 *Share the Olympic Dream*—Thematic Unit

#314 *Literature and Critical Thinking*

#418 *Julie of the Wolves*—Literature Unit

#495 *Focus on Women*

Answer Key

Page 13

Proclaim liberty throughout the land.

On Your Own (Suggested Answer) Two hundred ships from 30 nations filled the harbor, many of them tall ships. Giant fireworks displays lit up the night sky and the Statue of Liberty.

Page 17

1. 12.3 feet (3.75m)
2. 60 cents/gallon
3. 28,571
4. 83,333
5. $25,000,000
6. 1,714
7. 25%
8. about 83%
9. 30 months
10. 104 feet (31 m)
11. $1,190,000,000
12. 748

Page 21

1. a. 76–77 b. 70–73
2. a. 73–74 b. 74–75
3. a. $1.30 b. $1.05
4. a. 19 cents b. $3.09

Page 30

1. 1972; 17,998,810
2. 97%
3. 1,680,974
4. same; 538/547
5. 1976; 4,037,593
6. 44.%

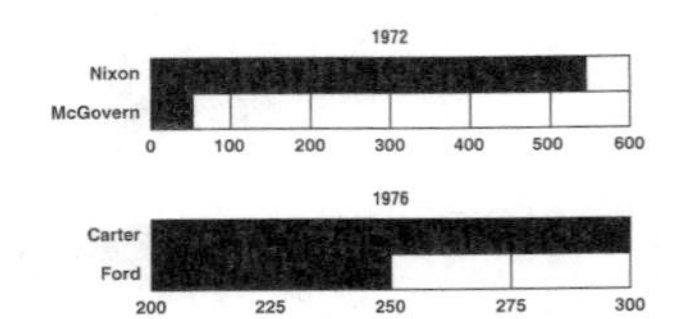

Page 33

1. b
2. a
3. f
4. d
5. g
6. e
7. h
8. c

Page 36

1. Nigeria
2. Algeria
3. Libya
4. Qatar
5. Saudi Arabia
6. Gabon
7. Iraq
8. Kuwait
9. Iran

Page 38

Gloria Steinem: Graduated from College, Worked in Journalism

Betty Friedan: Graduated from College, Worked in Journalism, Wrote One or More Books

Bella Abzug: Graduated from College, Promoted Equal Rights for Women, Was/Is Active in Politics, Served in Congress,

Shirley Chisholm: Graduated from College, Promoted Equal Rights for Women, Was/Is Active in Politics, Served in Congress,

Page 45

1. Obie, Tony
2. Tony, Oscar
3. Oscar, Emmy

Page 48

1. Roberto Clemente
2. Earl Anthony
3. Dorothy Hamill
4. Jack Nicklaus
5. Bobby Orr
6. Olga Korbut
7. Hanni Wenzel
8. Larry Csonka
9. Billie Jean King
10. Kip Keino

Page 51

1. 8
2. 12,400
3. 745
4. 380
5. 3,596
6. 247.68
7. 2.89
8. 18

Page 52

Check for appropriate responses.

Page 58

Osmonds: Mormon/first single was "One Bad Apple"/appeared regularly on TV/Alan, Wayne, Merrill, Jay, Donny/switched to country music/sister Marie was also a singer

Both: five brothers/ choreographed their dancing/all vocals/youngest member of the group was the most popular

Jacksons: signed with Motown/sisters Janet and LaToya were also singers/first single was "I Want You Back" /African American/ Jackie, Tito, Jermaine, Marlon, Michael

Page 66

1. Mark Spitz
2. Frank Shorter
3. Olga Korbut
4. Shane Gould
5. Kip Keino
6. Rick De Mont
7. Peggy Fleming
8. Karl Schranz
9. Nadia Comaneci
10. Bruce Jenner
11. Greg Louganis
12. Alberto Juantorena
13. Sugar Ray Leonard
14. Sheila Young
15. Franz Klammer
16. Irina Rodnina

Page 83

1. b
2. a
3. a
4. b
5. a
6. a
7. a
8. b
9. a
10. b
11. a
12. a
13. b
14. a
15. a
16. b
17. a
18. b
19. b
20. b
21. a
22. a
23. b
24. b
25. b

Page 84

Across

2. Hearst
4. Woodward
5. Steinem
7. Calley
10. Ali
11. Spitz
13. Gilmore
15. Blume
16. Jones
18. Abdul-Jabbar
19. Fixx

Down

1. Fawcett-Majors
3. Agnew
5. Spielberg
6. Mitchell
8. Knievel
9. Walters
12. King
14. Hendrix
17. Aaron

Page 85

1. 1977
2. 1970
3. 1973
4. 1971
5. 1978
6. 1979
7. 1975
8. 1971
9. 1974
10. 1976
11. 1977
12. 1972

Page 92

1. p
2. e
3. i
4. t
5. n
6. q
7. a
8. g
9. s
10. b
11. h
12. f
13. l
14. d
15. m
16. j
17. r
18. o
19. k
20. c